Nolan Ryan: Fireballer

About the Book

Here is the exciting life story of Nolan Ryan, a shy, honest country boy from Texas who struggled to become the most spectacular pitcher in baseball. In this close-up look the noted sportswriter Bill Libby shows how Nolan developed the best fastball in history, surpassing Sandy Koufax's major-league record for strikeouts in a single season and throwing four no-hitters in three seasons. Traded away by the Mets too soon and maturing with the Angels, Ryan thrills fans from New York to Los Angeles.

NOLAN RYAN
Fireballer

Bill Libby

G. P. Putnam's Sons • New York

Contents

*To David Combs, another fine young player
and another fine young man*

The author wishes to thank Nolan Ryan for all past interviews, his managers Matt Merola and Paul Goetz of Mattgo Enterprises in New York, and Bob Hood and Charles Mercer of Putnam's. He wishes to thank George Goodale, George Lederer, Ed Munson, and all the office staff, managers, coaches, and players around the Angels for all the help they have provided and always provide. And, finally, he wishes to thank Dick Miller and Melvin Durslag of the Los Angeles *Herald-Examiner*, Jeff Prugh and Ross Newhan of the Los Angeles *Times*, Don Merry of the Long Beach *Independent, Press-Telegram*, John Stellman of the Santa Ana *Register*, all the New York writers, broadcasters Dick Enberg, Don Drysdale, and Dave Niehaus, and all the writers and broadcasters who have contributed to the author's fund of knowledge about Nolan Ryan.

The Author

Bill Libby, the author of more than thirty books and many articles in national magazines, is a past winner of the U.S. National Magazine Sports Writer of the Year award. Among his recent popular sports biographies from Putnam's are *Willie Stargell: Baseball Slugger; Johnny Bench: The Little General; O.J.: The Story of Football's Fabulous O. J. Simpson.* Mr. Libby lives in Westminster, California, with his wife Sharon, and daughters, Allyson and Laurie.

1 Strikeout King

For a long time that season the strikeout record seemed just out of his reach, but Nolan Ryan went after it with all that he had left as the long season ran out.

The major-league record for strikeouts in a single season had been set by Sandy Koufax, the immortal left-hander who fanned 382 batters for the Los Angeles Dodgers in 1965. Now Nolan Ryan needed 16 strikeouts to surpass the standard in 1973.

This was Thursday night, September 26, and the campaign was almost over. Ryan had struck out 377 batters in 315 innings, and he was worn out. He had a sore right leg and a tired right arm.

Ryan was about to pitch against the Minnesota Twins in his home ball park, Anaheim Stadium, for the California Angels. If he had anything left and he was not injured, he could pitch with only two days' rest in the last game of the season on Sunday, but the Angels did not want to risk hurting the future of their spectacular twenty-six-year-old star.

"It may have to be tonight or never," he said as he left his pretty wife, Ruth, and young son, Reid, at their suburban house to go to the ball park. His wife would leave for the game later. "If I don't get close to the record tonight, I may never get another chance. The club doesn't want me to take any chances, even for a record. I wouldn't want to either. But I want the record."

He had been chasing it and a 20-victory record through the long last month of the season. The California club was completing a season that was disappointing in every respect except Ryan's performances. The Oakland A's already had clinched the American League's Western Division pennant. The Angels would finish fourth, losing four more games than they won. Only Nolan Ryan brightened the picture.

Nolan had thrown two no-hitters and two one-hitters. He had won his last six starts in a row to reach the 20-game victory mark. He had lost 16 for a light-hitting team that seldom offered him much support. The New York Mets had given up on the hard-throwing but wild and erratic youngster, but in his second season since being traded to the Angels, Ryan had matured to become one of the best pitchers in baseball.

At his best, he was the best. Still mastering a curveball and change-up which would give him a variety of pitches to confuse batters, he could overpower opponents with a fastball as fast as any pitcher had ever thrown one, a "live" thing which darted and dived and rose as it whistled past his nervous foes at the plate.

When he was getting his "hard one" across the plate, the batters were beaten.

There were more polished pitchers around, who had more experience, better control and were more consistent, but none was more dazzling than this developing superstar. He might be knocked out of the box one game but pitch a no-hitter the next game. He had become the sort of pitcher who was good far more often than he was bad. He had proved to be the sort of pitcher who comes along about once in a decade, who was almost impossible to hit when he was right.

Sandy Koufax was the last one like that, and now there was Nolan Ryan. No other pitcher in the game would have been a fair bet to get 16 strikeouts in two games, much less one, but it was something Nolan could do. He'd struck out 17 batters in a game twice— once the year before and once this year. But he had worked in 40 games, throwing more pitches per game than any other pitcher in the game, and the odds were against him now.

He drove through Orange County to the stadium, took the elevator down to the basement, and walked through the cool dark corridors to the team's dressing room. He took off his sports clothes and dressed in his white home flannels, number 30, with the blue and red trim, the blue, long-sleeved undershirt with the red "Angels" across the front, and the blue cap with the red bill. He sat by his locker awhile, his long fingers gently rubbing his sore right leg. He doesn't look like a power pitcher. He is slender but has heavy legs. He pushes off hard with his right leg when he pitches, and he puts a tremendous strain on it.

He studied the fingers on his right hand, his pitching

hand. As a boy he had cut the thumb and forefinger opening a coffee can. The cut never was stitched together properly. The flesh healed itself but remained sensitive. Pitching, he developed blisters, which bothered him a great deal. For a while he took the advice of a trainer and soaked his fingers in pickle brine in an effort to toughen them. Now he filed down the hard skin until it was ready to bleed but did not often blister.

He rubbed his elbow with snake oil. He often hunted and caught the snakes himself. He was a country boy, born in the small town of Refugio, Texas, and reared in nearby Alvin, where he still lived on a ranch in the winter between seasons. He has a lot of the country boy about him, a small-town Texan who never seems far from farm or ranch.

He is a handsome young man with short brown hair, brown eyes, and a boyish face. He speaks slowly in Southwestern accents. He is proud of his performances but not boastful about them. He is soft-spoken, not loud. He is not given to loud clothes or long hair. He is a sort of old-fashioned young man, very straight and sincere, extremely well liked by other players, the press, and the public.

"I would like the strikeout record, yes, I would," he said softly to a reporter. "I want to win most of all, but now that I have won twenty this season, which is what I wanted, I would like the strikeout record, too. But I'm tired, and I don't know how many strikeouts I have left in my arm. It's been an unbelievable season for me with the no-hitters and the near no-hitters and the twenty victories, and I'd like the strikeout record, too, since I'm so close, but I don't want to take any chances with my future going for it."

His expression was serious. He looked a bit drawn and tired. He said, "It's been a long season and a hard season for the team. If we were going for the pennant and the play-offs and the World Series, well, we'd be lifted up by it and inspired by it and wouldn't feel worn out, but we're not going anywhere, and we feel it. This is a personal thing for me, this record, but I wouldn't be this close without the help of my teammates. I know they want it for me and want to help me get it."

He shook his head slightly and concluded, "I've been feeling the pressure a little lately. The record's so close, yet so far away. Everyone's rooting for me, it seems. I don't want to disappoint anyone. I don't want to be disappointed myself. It hasn't been easy getting to this point, and I don't want to let it get away now. But all I can do is my best and hope for the best. It's not going to be easy."

He got up and went out on the field to warm up. It was twilight, and the fans were moving into their seats excitedly. It would not be a big crowd, but it would be an excited one. There would be close to 10,000 fans in the big ball park, but there would not be half that many if Ryan were not hurling. They were there in hope he would reach the record, although almost everyone thought he would have to finish it off two days later.

As it grew dark, the banks of artificial lights illuminated the grass field. Lights blinked on the scoreboard topped with a towering *A,* ringed with a halo. It was a hot night, heavy with humidity.

Minnesota moved in a veteran team with some of the greatest hitters in the game—Rod Carew, Tony Oliva and Harmon Killebrew, for example. Carew was hitting .350 and on his way to his third American

League batting crown and second in succession. Oliva, a three-time league batting champion, was close to .300 this time. Killebrew had been hurt and had little time left at the top, but he was among the all-time lifetime leaders with more than 500 home runs. He remained a dangerous slugger. Others in the Twins' lineup posed serious threats to Ryan.

Nolan seemed tight at the start, and it seemed unlikely he would get very far, which would have ended all hopes for a record. It seemed certain he needed 10 or more strikeouts this night to have a chance to get the others when he worked with little rest Sunday.

The first batter, center fielder Steve Brye, ripped a single. Second baseman Carew walked, moving Brye to second. Designated hitter Oliva singled him home. First baseman Killebrew drove a double to bring in the other two. Swifly, Ryan and the Angels trailed, 3–0.

There was no one out when Angel manager Bobby Winkles went worriedly out to talk to Ryan, while relief pitchers warmed up hurriedly in the Angel bullpen. Ryan was wild, throwing bad balls, getting behind the batters three and oh, three and one, three and two, and having to come in with a good pitch they could hit. He was trying too hard and was without his natural rhythm. Winkles reminded Nolan he didn't have to overthrow to throw hard.

The manager decided to let Nolan throw to at least one more batter before removing him. If he could get into the groove, a reliever might not be necessary. Nolan stood on the mound, trying to get his thinking straight. Then he went to work. He threw strikes to right fielder Jim Holt, who watched the third one streak by for the first "K" of the night in the scorebooks and the first roar from the crowd. Then Nolan threw strikes to catcher George Mitterwald, who went out swinging on the third one, which brought another roar from the crowd.

Nolan missed on some pitches to third baseman Eric Soderholm and walked him to put two men on with two out. But then he blazed three past left fielder Mike Adams, who took the last one to wind up the inning at last. The fans applauded, but Ryan and the Angels went back to the dugout behind by three runs.

Five minutes later his teammates had got the runs back for him. Dave Goltz, a husky, towering right-hander from Pelican Rapids, Minnesota, a promising rookie pitcher for the Twins, had his troubles at the start, too. Center fielder Mickey Rivers beat out an infield hit. Shortstop Dave Chalk singled. Designated hitter Frank Robinson, the great veteran, singled in the first run. First baseman Tom McCraw walked to load the bases. Right fielder Vada Pinson flied to center, Shaw scoring after the catch. Left fielder Ken Berry grounded out, but Robinson brought home the tying run on the throw to first. By the time Al Gallagher, the third baseman, had grounded out to end the inning the rivals were even.

Starting fresh, Ryan got shortstop Jerry Terrell to ground out. Leadoff batter Brye slapped a single, but Nolan's fast one was steaming now, and he got Carew and Oliva on swinging third strikes to end the second session. The Angels went out one, two, three in their half, too. The other hurler had steadied down, too.

After Killebrew walked, Holt took a called third strike in the third. Mitterwald reached base on an error by Billy Parker at second, but Soderholm grounded into a double play, short to second to first, to finish off the inning.

Chalk singled, went to third on a wild pitch, and scored on McCraw's single in the Angel half to put the home team in front, 4–3, before Goltz got out of the inning.

Ryan takes an enormous stride with his left leg as he rears far back, braces hard on his right leg, and hurls the ball overhand to the plate. He'd found the range now, and his ball was bursting past the batters and smacking loudly into catcher Jeff Torborg's glove before the hitters could react strongly.

Nolan struck out the side in the fourth, blazing called third strikes past Adams and Terrell, then getting a hopping hard one past Brye's swinging bat. The crowd was reacting to every strikeout now, roaring enthusiastically. He had eight strikeouts after four innings. He was hot, and the record was within reach.

Nolan seemed to peak in the fifth when he got Carew swinging for his fourth consecutive strikeout. Carew is no free-swinging slugger. He is a master with the stick in his hand. He usually gets wood on a pitch when he goes for it. He seldom strikes out. But Ryan had now struck him out two times in a row.

Another master batsman, Oliva, who had struck out his previous time up, got wood on a Ryan pitch this time and singled. But then the free-swinging slugger Killebrew struck out swinging. Holt flied out to finish the inning. Although it was an easy out, the crowd groaned. The only way the fans wanted the Twins to go out was by striking out.

The Angels went out in order in the fourth and fifth.

But the Twins struck in the sixth. Mitterwald was safe when Gallagher erred at third. Soderholm flied out, but Adams walked, moving Mitterwald to second. Terrell singled him home. Brye bounced into a double play, but the damage had been done, and the score was even again.

Ryan seemed to be starting to tire. The long season and the strain of throwing hard on every pitch, trying to strike out every batter, were beginning to tell on him. Also, his sore right leg was cramping up. "It hurt a lot every time I pushed off it," he admitted later.

He bent his back and went at it. He hadn't pitched a strikeout in the sixth, so had fallen behind the record pace. He got strikeouts on every out in the seventh to catch up again. He whiffed Carew for the third straight time, catching him looking at a blazer called a strike by home plate umpire Red Flaherty. After he walked Oliva, Ryan struck out Killebrew, swinging, for the second straight time. After Holt singled to put two on, Ryan struck out Mitterwald, swinging, to shut off the surge.

After Mitterwald missed on the third strike, the crowd came to their feet to give Ryan a standing ovation. They were thrilled. He had fanned 14 in seven frames and now needed only 1 strikeout to tie the record and 2 to surpass it. There was a tremendous amount of excitement in the outdoor arena as a sweating, tired Ryan went wearily back to the dugout to rest up for the following inning. He was not smiling. He was working too hard, concentrating too hard. The game was not yet won, the record not yet his.

Parker singled in the home half, but it was wasted, and the Angels went out without scoring, so the tie

19

stood. The 9,100 fans stood and hollered at Ryan as he trotted to the mound to start the eighth. He started it smoking. Right-handed batter Soderholm fouled the first pitch back for the first strike. He took a low pitch which was called a ball, booed by the crowd. He took another ball to more boos. He fouled the next pitch back to even the count at two and two.

He stepped out of the batter's box, trying to gather himself. Ryan studied him intently, on the verge of the record. The batter went back into the box, and the pitcher bent in to take the signal from the catcher. Ryan threw, and Soderholm swung and connected and sent the ball sailing high toward the right-field seats along the foul line. Just before it reached the seats, it curved foul. The fans sighed their obvious relief.

Ryan tried a curve. It broke high. "Ball three," umpire Flaherty hollered. The crowd booed, as it did every ball. If it were up to the Angel fans, each of Ryan's pitches would have been called a strike. Ryan threw a fastball high. Too high. Ball four. The batter walked as the fans groaned.

Ryan was laboring now. It was work now, hard work. Adams stepped in. Ryan threw to him hard. Too hard. The ball got away from Nolan and went wild, inside, past the catcher's grasp as the batter went sprawling to avoid being hit by the blazer. The base runner raced to second. On the next pitch Adams drew back and reached out and just got his bat on the ball and grounded to second. It was an easy out, but there was only mild applause. The fans wanted those strikeouts. Terrell grounded to second to mild applause for the second out.

Steve Brye moved in to bat. Ryan, his uniform

soaked with sweat, studied him. The batter swung at the first pitch and missed it, and the crowd roared. Brye swung at the second pitch and missed it, and the crowd roared louder. The base runner had broken for second on the pitch. Torborg threw to the base. It was close. The umpire there spread his hands, palms down. The runner was safe. Amazingly, the Angel fans cheered. With two strikes on the batter, they did not want Minnesota retired on the base paths.

Ryan throws a lot of pitches. All wild pitchers who go for strikeouts do. It takes them three, four, five, six, or more pitches to retire batters. They walk many. They do not get many on first pitches which are bounced into the infield or flied to the outfield. Ryan had thrown a lot of pitches this season and a lot this night, and even with no balls and two strikes on the batter he was not about to waste one. He reared back and threw as hard as he could, and the batter, Brye, swung at it and missed it, and the crowd came to their feet screaming. With his fifteenth strikeout of the game, Ryan had tied the record of 382 for the season. He tipped his cap as he trotted to the dugout with a faint suggestion of a smile on his face.

In the last of the eighth Rivers singled, Shaw popped to first, Rivers stole, and Robinson walked to put two on. But McCraw struck out, and Pinson flied out to finish off the threat, and as the teams went to the ninth inning, the contest was still tied at 4–4.

Nolan needed one more "K" to set the record, but it would not be an easy one to get. His right leg hurt horribly now, and trainer Freddie Frederico and team physician Dr. Jules Rasinski were in the dugout working on the leg while the team batted. When the team went out, Ryan went out to pitch the ninth.

Ryan's first pitch to Carew was a ball. His second was a strike, called, the crowd hollering. Carew swung on the next pitch, but he was late on it and got only a little piece of it, and he fouled it back to the stands as the fans hollered. Two strikes. One to go. Ryan blazed a ball just outside. Ball two, called to boos. Ryan threw again, and Carew got a little piece of it and fouled it off third. Ryan threw again, and Carew popped it in the air to second. One out.

Oliva came up. Ball one. Then strike one, a foul just off first. Then strike two, a foul back of the plate. Again, Nolan was within one strike. He went for it, but Oliva got his bat on the ball. He got around late but slashed a foul into the stands off third. The fans waited expectantly. Ryan pitched, and Oliva popped the ball to short, and the fans groaned again.

Killebrew came up. The first pitch missed outside. Ball one. The second pitch was off speed, designed to surprise the slugger. It did. He started to swing, held up, heard the pitch called strike one. Nervously, Nolan walked around the rubber, rubbing up the ball. Twice he walked forward to smooth off the ground around the rubber with his spikes. Then he threw low for ball two. Catcher Torborg went out to talk to him in an effort to steady him down. But it was more a matter of Nolan's hurting now than it was of anything else.

Torborg returned to the plate, and Ryan threw. He threw low for ball three. His throwing motion seemed labored now. Trainer Frederico ran out to talk to him to make sure he was not experiencing any unreasonable pain. The crowd booed a bit, not wanting the Angels

22

to take Ryan out, but his health was the team's main concern. Frederico got Ryan's word he was all right and returned to the dugout. Ryan threw a little easier, and Killebrew clubbed it into center for a single. Rich Reese came on to run for him.

Holt moved in. Ball one. A foul to left for strike one. And then a fly to left for the third out, which brought groans from the crowd. The game was tied, but the ending of an enemy rally on a fly ball brought groans because the crowd did not want the game to end without Ryan's breaking the record.

It was apparent in the Angel half that the home crowd didn't want the home team to score to win the game because the game would then have been ended without the record for Ryan. Berry bounced a single into center. Gallagher hit into a double play, and the fans cheered. Gallagher growled, returning to the dugout. Parker flied out to center, and the crowd cheered. The Angels shook their heads in amazement, then took the field for the tenth.

The question then was would Ryan return to pitch the tenth! A reliever was warming up in the bullpen. Ryan did not emerge from the dugout when he was due. It seemed then the team would pull him to protect his arm, and the crowd buzzed uneasily. Actually, the Angels were stalling while the trainer and doctor massaged Ryan's cramped leg. Manager Winkles admitted later, "I thought about taking him out, but he insisted he was all right, so I let him go out there."

Ryan ran out, and a relieved crowd yelled happily. But many heard announcer Dick Enberg report on their hand-held transistor radios that not only would this probably be his last inning, but by working into extra innings, Nolan had almost certainly eliminated himself from working any innings at all on the last day of the season. It certainly seemed now or never.

Mitterwald was the first batter. The first pitch to him was outside, a called ball one. The second pitch was fouled back for strike one. The next pitch was low and outside for ball two. Winkles watched intently as the batter bounced a single into left. Soderholm, the only Twin starter who hadn't struck out, was next up.

Since tying the record, Ryan had faced five batters without striking one out. The first pitch to Soderholm missed for ball one. The next one was bounced over first, but it was ruled foul to the relief of the fans. The next pitch missed for ball two, and Winkles seemed to lean half out the dugout, debating whether to remove his tired hurler. Ryan threw, and the hitter bounced the ball to second baseman Parker, who turned it into a double play.

Frederico and Torborg went out to Ryan again to ask him again how he felt. He said he was all right, and they returned to their posts. Adams came up. He had struck out twice. He took a high pitch which was called a strike, and he shook his head angrily about it. He took another high one, but this one was called a ball. Ryan's next throw was low for ball two, which brought boos. His next one was outside for ball three, which brought more boos. The pitcher walked around worriedly. Then he bent back in and threw, and the batter hit it into center for a single.

Terrell stepped up. Ryan's first pitch was wild. When catcher Torborg threw the ball back to Nolan, the pitcher dropped it. He bent down wearily to get it. The tension was getting to him now. He was terribly tired, too. And his leg was aching awfully, he admitted later. But he didn't want to give up. It meant too much to him. So he took a chance. And they let him take the chance. Ryan threw a second ball. Then a strike down the middle. Then another strike that the batter popped to center.

Well, that was probably it. If the Angels did not end it in their half, Ryan surely would not be permitted to pitch another half inning. Behind home plate a proud but disappointed Ruth Ryan was signing autographs for those of Nolan's young fans who recognized her.

The Angels went down in order in the last of the tenth. They took the field to start the eleventh. No one went to the mound at first. A reliever continued to labor in the bullpen. The trainer and doctor continued to labor on Ryan's leg in the dugout. The crowd waited expectantly, hoping Nolan would come out to pitch one more inning. "He wanted it, so I decided to give him one more," manager Winkles said later. Ryan trotted out, and the crowd hollered happily about it.

He had not struck out anyone the last two innings. The first batter, Brye, took a ball, then a strike. Then he fouled one back. For the third time Ryan was within one strike of his record, and the fans were roaring. Brye swung and seemed to miss, and the fans jumped up, cheering, but it turned out he had nicked the pitch, and it was a foul which flew back past Torborg's desperate grab. On the next pitch the batter popped to short for the first out.

Nolan was still throwing hard but not smoking them over as he had earlier. He was struggling tiredly now as Carew came up. Ryan threw a called ball, a called strike. Then ball two. Ball three. Ball four. Carew

25

walked, and Winkles went out to talk to Ryan with the crowd booing him every step of the way. He was cheered when he went back to the dugout without taking Ryan out. But he had told him he was about out of time.

Everyone knew then that this at last really was it. If Ryan survived this inning, he would not be back for another. And now he would not be back on Sunday. "I had two outs to get my record strikeout," Ryan recalled later. "I didn't want to settle for a tie. That would have been worse than not getting it at all, somehow. I was right up against it then, and I knew it, and I felt it, and it was hard to handle."

Everyone in the ball park watched intently as the slender hurler bent to his task with the lead run leading off first and the awesome Oliva up. Ryan put everything into every pitch. He was inside with his first one for ball one. He was outside with his second for ball two. He'd missed on five straight pitches now. He walked around, trying to pull himself together. He threw a rocket. Oliva went for it and missed it, twisting around with the force of his swing. Strike one. Ryan threw Oliva a second strike, but he hit this one to center, where it was caught for the second out.

One out left now. The pressure pounded at the pitcher. And at the batter, Reese, who had replaced Killebrew and came up now. He was the twelfth batter to come up since Ryan had struck one out. And the fiftieth batter to come up since Ryan had started the contest. Ryan had thrown 325 innings this season and more than 200 pitches this game. What did he have left? He reached for the record now for the very last time.

Ryan gave it everything he had left. He wound up, pulled the ball far back, drove down hard on his sore right leg, reached far out with his left leg, and whipped his right arm around, firing the pitch plateward. Reese swung and missed, and the fans screamed. Again Ryan wound up, reared back, and threw with all his might. Again Reese swung and missed, and again the fans screamed. But the base runner broke for second. Torborg threw. As it was earlier, this one was close. Again the runner was ruled safe to the cheers of the home fans.

Nolan Ryan shook his head and walked around the mound nervously. Finally, he took his place, his spikes on the slab. He took his signal from the crafty catcher, Torborg. But craft didn't enter into it this time. The signal would be for a fastball. Reese knew it. Everyone knew it. And Ryan threw it. He did not waste it; he threw it with all his might across the plate. And Reese ripped at it, bringing his bat around hard. And missed it. As the batter twisted off-balance, the pitch thudded into the catcher's mitt, the umpire's thumb went skyward, and bedlam erupted in the arena.

With his 16th strikeout of the night and record-setting 383d of the season, Nolan Ryan turned around in delight and relief as his teammates came screaming out of the dugout to shake his hand and pound his back and shout their congratulations to him and to escort him back to the dugout as the fans stood and hollered themselves hoarse at their happiness. The fans wouldn't stop. For nearly five minutes they stood and yelled happily until an embarrassed Ryan reluctantly stepped outside the dugout to wave his appreciation for the ovation.

Only then could the contest continue. And it was as if his teammates had been waiting for him to get the record before they went out to get the game. McCraw's single, an error, and sub Richie Scheinblum's double finished off the foes fast in the last of the eleventh, and the Angels had won, 5–4, for Ryan's twenty-first triumph of the season. The fans didn't want to go home but stood and cheered a final standing ovation for a long time as Nolan Ryan, the new strikeout king of baseball, returned to the dressing room.

2 Growing Up

Lynn Nolan Ryan, Jr., was born January 31, 1947. His father, Lynn Nolan Ryan, Sr., was called Lynn. He and Nolan's mother did not want him to be called Junior, so they started calling him by his middle name early, and it stuck.

They were living at the time in Woodsboro, Texas, a town so small Mrs. Ryan had to go to the county seat of Refugio to have her son born in a hospital. They later moved to Alvin and it was in this town of 12,000 about twenty miles from Houston that Nolan went through his teens, met the girl he would marry, and settled with her on a ranch.

About 15 miles from the Gulf of Mexico, Alvin is a hot, humid Texas town. It is a sprawling little town full of old white frame and newer brick houses, and everyone seems to know everyone else there. Many of the residents in the area earn their livings at cattle ranching or farming, and there are rice fields outside town. Many men go outside town to work in the chemical or oil companies in Galveston and Freeport or for NASA in Houston. But it is not a wealthy town. People live simply here. They hunt or fish and have to go to the big city for a big night out.

Alvin was named for Alvin Morgan, the storekeeper who settled it and whose store, now Stanton's, stands where it has been for more than fifty years. There is a sign in the store which says the proprietor will pay 1 percent of his receipts to the church or charity of the customer's choice. The largest sign on the main street, Gordon Street, reads, DRIVE FRIENDLY. Many of the streets are named for Confederate Civil War heroes —Lee, Hood, Gordon, and so forth.

The youngest member of his family, Nolan was in the first grade when they moved to the brick bungalow on Dezo Street where his mother still lives (his father died in 1971). Growing up, Nolan could hear the whistle of the Santa Fe trains as they passed nearby. The basketball hoop where he shot his first field goals still hangs from the house.

Off-seasons now Nolan goes to throw baseballs against the brick wall in the schoolyard at Alvin High, where his sister Judy is a math teacher. All four of his sisters were to become schoolteachers, and three married schoolteachers. Judy married an electrician. Nolan married Ruth Holdorff, who grew up in an old white frame house on shady Adoue Street, two blocks from the high school. She was called the prettiest girl in school. She is a beautiful young woman, and she and Nolan are happy to return here every winter.

"I like small-town living," he says. "I like open spaces and open roads and clean air and peacefulness.

30

I like knowing my neighbors. I like the feel of farm life and animals. I like to hunt and fish." In his early life, his ambition was to be a veterinarian.

Nolan was the youngest of six children. His father was a supervisor for a petroleum company, who worked hard in the oilfields every day. To help support his family, he delivered the Houston *Post* evenings. Nolan used to help out. He says, "I think I may have developed my strong wrists rolling five hundred to one thousand newspapers every night. I worked at it from the second grade on."

He laughs and adds, "I'd like to say I developed my strong pitching arm throwing the newspapers onto front porches, but by the time I was a teenager of fourteen and in high school I was driving a car while delivering the papers, and I'd steer with my right arm and throw with my left arm. I was as wild left-handed as I was right-handed. I scattered those newspaper all over. I even knocked out a few streetlights."

An older brother, who became a career man in the Army, played a big part in developing him, Nolan recalls.

He remembers: "I was wild from the first time I tried to throw a ball. When I was five, I couldn't hit my brother from five feet away. He was six years older than I was and a fair athlete, and he had as much to do with my career as anyone. He helped me a lot. Sometimes a boy that much older might not pay much attention to a kid brother, but he took time to play catch with me and teach me and encourage me in sports. As a result, I started playing in the Little League when I was eight years old, which was a year or two before a lot of the other kids started. I was a real veteran when

I finished my Little League career five years later. I was an all-star shortstop my last year, but I liked to pitch best."

Nolan played almost all the positions as a Little Leaguer. He pitched because the coaches discovered he could throw harder than most kids, but he was also wild. He hit hard, too, and fielded well and was moved around wherever he was needed. He was taller than many of the other kids, but skinny.

He began to develop an ambition to be a baseball player. He says, "I don't believe in premonitions, but I remember having one. That was in the Little League. We were beaten in a district tournament and were lined up on the field for the award ceremonies. We were feeling pretty low. Some former major leaguer—I can't remember his name—was passing out the awards. He said, 'One of you boys is going to be a major leaguer someday.' I thought at the time I would be that boy."

When he was graduated from the Little League, his brother suggested it was time he concentrated on one position. Nolan recalls, "My brother pinned me down and asked me where I wanted to play. I told him I wanted to pitch because a pitcher gets more involved in a game than anyone else. From that time on he did everything possible to keep me pitching, even to him in the yard at home. He warned me not to fool around with sidearm and three-quarter pitches because using more than one motion might put a strain on my arm which would hurt it, so I threw straight overhead, and I've never really had any serious arm problems. It helped me a lot."

When he started high school, Nolan also played football and basketball. He liked all sports, but he was outweighed by bigger boys in football. He remembers when he was a 150-pounder in the ninth grade and playing against Norm Bulaich, who weighed 195 pounds. Bulaich, who became a pro runner for the Baltimore Colts, was a 9.5 sprinter starring for nearby La Marque High.

Nolan recalls, "He took the ball on the first play and went up the middle. I was a defensive back and the last guy with a shot at him. I hit him, and when I looked up, he was going over the goal line and there were cleat marks all over me. So much for football."

He was better at basketball. He hit his top height of six-two early, could shoot, and played center. He was a scoring star for a team which compiled a fine 27–4 record in each of his junior and senior seasons. He was selected All-State as a senior and was invited to visit the campuses of some small colleges in the area but got into baseball before he could get any firm scholarship offers.

"I really wanted to go to college, play basketball, and study to be a veterinarian," he admits. "But my parents had already put four kids through college and weren't that well off financially. A baseball bonus was hard to turn down."

As a boy, Ryan rooted for the Houston Astros, the home team in that area. He remembers: "I never asked an athlete for an autograph. It never dawned on me to do so. I didn't see many. I saved baseball cards, but I never thought of sending them off the way the kids do now and getting them autographed. I get a lot of cards sent to me now for my autograph, but I never did anything like that when I was a boy. I did dream of playing for the Houston team. But it was just a dream. Most boys dream of making the majors when they grow up. With most it never comes to anything. With me it wasn't a burning ambition or anything. I did like to pitch, but I didn't really think I was good enough to make the majors someday."

He did go to see the great Sandy Koufax pitch for the Dodgers in Houston one day in 1965, Nolan's senior season. That was the year Koufax set the single-season strikeout record at 382. Koufax won 26 games and lost 8 that year and won 27 and lost 9 the next year before he retired with a chronic elbow ailment.

"I don't think I will ever see a pitcher as good as Koufax," Ryan recalls. "His fastball did things I never thought a ball could be made to do."

In high school Ryan didn't try to develop a curve or change up speeds much because he didn't have to do so to get batters out. "I had a good fastball. I more or less reared back and let it go," he says. "I didn't try to throw to spots. I aimed only to get it across the plate. I didn't know any of the weaknesses of batters. You didn't see them enough. I wasn't that smart. I wasn't a pitcher. I was a thrower. I wasn't as wild as I was later because I wasn't aiming at spots. I was just trying to get it around the plate. The batters swung wildly at a lot of bad balls anyway."

His senior season he won 20 games and lost only 4. He led his team into the state tournament and hurled a no-hit game during the tournament. He was selected to the All-State team, but his team did not win the tournament, and he did not win over many scouts. His record was such that scouts from most of the major-league teams came to see him pitch schoolboy ball, but they were not sure of him.

John Robert "Red" Murff, a Texan who made it to

the majors as a relief pitcher with the Milwaukee Braves in 1965 and 1966, was the scout who cost the world a good animal doctor and gave it a great baseball pitcher. He started scouting Nolan during his sophomore year and stayed with him.

"He was wild and unpolished and not built very big, but I thought he had a pitcher's arm and a good attitude, and I was convinced he was worth taking," Murff later recalled. He sent glowing reports on Ryan back to New York and eventually talked Met general manager Bing Devine into flying into Texas to scout the youngster personally.

"Murff and Devine showed up at the park on a day I wasn't even supposed to pitch," Ryan remembers. "So there's a conference between Murff and my high school coach, who finally agrees to let me start though I've only had two days' rest. I probably had my worst game of the year.

"The team we were playing was terrible-looking. They were a real small school with just a sandlot for a field, without lights or a fence or anything. And I was really wild. Couldn't get anything over the plate, and when I did get one across, they hit it pretty good.

"To top it off, we were losing about three to one in the fourth inning when I came up with the bases loaded and nobody out. The coach called a squeeze bunt, and I popped up—into a triple play. As I was walking back to the bench to get my glove, I saw Devine getting up and leaving the park. I figured that was the end of it."

It wasn't, however.

When the Mets got to Houston, Ryan was invited to work out with them before a game at the Astrodome. Met pitcher Tug McGraw says, "I won't forget that, and neither will the guy catching him. It was Johnny Stephenson and Nolan was humming that fastball in there pretty good. I think Stephenson either wants a curveball but forgets to call for it, or he calls for one and Nolan doesn't know how to throw one yet. Anyway, Stephenson is crouched down, waiting for the ball to break; only it doesn't. It just comes sailing right along. It broke Stephenson's collarbone, and he's still got a big lump on it to this day."

Yogi Berra, the great former catcher, who was coaching for the club, took over as catcher while general manager Devine, field manager Casey Stengel, and others observed.

Devine noted, "He really threw hard." In his inimitable way, Stengel observed, "He threw so fast I couldn't see his pitch, so I figgered he was all right. What you can't see in a pitcher you got to like." Berra recalls, "He was a skinny kid, thirty, forty pounds lighter than later, and he threw just as fast as he did later." He was asked what he thought when he caught his first fastball from Ryan. Berra's brow creased in thought. Then he remembered. Grinning, he said, "I thought: Sign him."

The Mets did. The way they talked at the time Nolan got carried away and figured they'd draft him the first chance they got. They did not go that far. But other teams did not go as far.

That was the first year of the free-agent draft in which the major-league pros had to gain rights to the amateurs in high school and college ranks by picking them in turn instead of being able to take anyone they could sign. Proof that baseball scouts fall far short of perfection came when team after team picked players through round after round before the Mets made Nolan

Ryan, an eighteen-year-old right-handed pitcher from a high school in Alvin, Texas, the 295th player chosen out of the grab bag. If that year's draft could be held again this year, there are at least 294 lads who would not again be selected ahead of Nolan Ryan.

At the time Ryan was disappointed. "I was selected so far down the line I figured they figured there wasn't much hope for me," he says. "However, the Mets did offer me a twenty-thousand-dollar bonus to sign. That was a lot of money to offer a kid drafted as late as I was. I wasn't much interested in money, but my father told me not to turn it down."

Nolan's dad died in 1971 of lung cancer. He did get to see his son make the majors but was gone before his boy became a big star. This saddens Nolan, who has invested his baseball money in ranchland around Alvin on which he plans someday to breed cattle. He returns with his wife and son there every winter to tend his spread and hunt and fish and enjoy the sort of life he knew growing up. He even got to college, attending Alvin Junior College with his wife during off-seasons. But in June, 1965, Nolan Ryan became a baseball player professionally, and it was the end of his boyhood and the beginning of his manhood.

3 Moving Up in the Minors

Turning pro in the Mets' minor-league season, eighteen-year-old Nolan Ryan was assigned to Marion, Virginia, in the Appalachian League, a rookie league in which newly signed youngsters could complete the season.

The plane ride he took to the Southeast was his first. He'd never even been more than a few miles from home before. "I'm not the type of person who meets people real well. I was lonely. I felt lost. I was scared to death. I was homesick. I wanted to go home the whole time I was there," he remembers.

"Marion was like a gold-rush town. They hadn't even finished building the ball park yet. I never realized how bad the minors were until later when I got to the majors. I didn't know the hardships were hardships until later when I looked back on them. To me at the time it was just a new experience.

"The clubhouse had no room to stand, much less dress, two showers, no hot water. We used dirty uniforms. There were forty-one guys on the club, and on road trips we'd have guys standing in the aisles. We went by bus. We couldn't afford anything better.

"Most of the teams in the Mets' minor-league system were set by midseason, and this was the only place they had to put the new kids and some of the overflow. Seventy-some players passed through during the season. There were forty-one when I was there.

"The manager didn't have much time to teach me about pitching. He spent most of his time listening to guys complain because he wasn't playing them. I'll tell you, if you got to play at all with that many guys to choose from, you had a chance to make the majors."

Clearly, Ryan could throw hard, so he got to pitch. But he made a lot of bad pitches. He walked a lot of men. He made a lot of wild pitches. He got into thirteen games and pitched seventy-eight innings. He struck out 115 but walked 56. He tied for the league lead in hitting batters, hitting eight.

The hard-throwing youngster had the hitters nervous. They were afraid he'd hit someone in the head and really hurt him. But he was as likely to hit someone in the stands with a pitch as he was the man at the plate. He'd put men on bases and wild-pitch them along. He didn't know how to hold them on the bases, so they stole a lot on him. He didn't know how to field his position.

Ryan would get in trouble and have to come across with a pitch. Sometimes one hit would beat him. Opponents scored 47 times on him on only 61 hits. He had a mediocre earned run average of 4.38 runs per game. He won only three decisions and lost six. He was deeply disappointed with the experience.

However, he was sent that winter to an instructional league where Eddie Stanky was assigned to tutor him. A scrappy former big-league ballplayer and manager, Stanky knew the game and got along well with Ryan. Nolan says, "I think he probably taught me as much baseball as anybody." Stanky adds, "He had a lot to learn, but he wanted to learn. He was willing to listen, and he worked hard. I wasn't a pitcher, but I could see this kid could be one of the best. He just needed polishing. He had more ability than other kids his age."

Records weren't kept of the players in that instructional league, but Ryan improved rapidly, and by the time he returned to Texas for the last part of the winter he had regained much of his enthusiasm for the sport.

He was assigned to the Mets' Class A Western Carolina League team at Greenville, South Carolina, at the start of the 1966 season. He was a year older at nineteen and had endured his first experience far from home in pro ball and was better prepared for the rugged life of the minors.

He had also added a little polish and knew a little more about how to pitch. He'd gained a few pounds and was throwing harder than ever. He threw too hard for Class A opposition. Few of the players there had his ability or potential.

He pitched in 29 games and worked 183 innings. He led the league with 28 starts, with 17 victories, with 272 strikeouts and also with 127 walks. He was second in shutouts with 5. He struck out 19 in nine innings in one game. He had an excellent earned run average of

2.51. He lost only 2 decisions. With his 17–2 record he was voted Pitcher of the Year in that circuit.

"I picked up a lot of confidence that season. It meant a lot to my future. I began to think maybe it wouldn't be so tough after all. I began to think maybe it would be easy. I didn't know how tough it would get. I was just ahead of the others there. But I was about to move up to more advanced leagues where others would be ahead of me," he has said.

He was a sensation, and as the reports arrived in the Mets' offices in New York, they got excited about him there. The brass wanted to take a look at him. But the Western Carolina League season ended on August 20, and by the rules a major-league team could not call up a player at that point until September 1, so Nolan was sent to Williamsport, Pennsylvania, in the Eastern League while he was waiting.

He got into three games there, lost two of them, and didn't win any. He struck out 35 and walked 12 in nineteen innings and gave up less than one earned run per nine innings, but he beat himself a couple of times. He struck out 21 Pawtucket, Rhode Island, batters in ten innings in one game and lost it, 2–1. "Two guys stole home on me," he admitted later, laughing ruefully. It was a league record anyway.

He moved up to the Mets nervously. "Scared to death is the way to put it," he says now with a laugh. He was not laughing then. No Met was laughing. But they were being laughed at. They were baseball's biggest joke. After finishing tenth their first five seasons, they had risen only slightly to ninth in the sixth season. It wasn't enough for the press and public, who were running out of patience with their expansionists.

41

Their manager, Casey Stengel, had been fired, and the new manager, Wes Westrum, had been under fire all season. Everyone was disgusted with another dreary year of being beaten and ridiculed. Later Ryan remembered, "I know what it's like to be a rookie on a club of veterans. I wasn't accepted. I felt lost."

Nolan says, "I was called up because I had a good arm, but I didn't know what to do with it. No curve. Couldn't get the ball over. No rhythm. Never delivered the ball the same way twice."

He was sent into his first big-league game in the seventh inning of a game against Atlanta. He pitched against Rico Carty, Henry Aaron, Ed Mathews, Felipe Alou, and Joe Torre, who were among the best batters in baseball. He gave up a home run to Torre, walked one, and struck out the others. He threw nothing but fastballs. Aaron later observed, "Hey, that kid can hum that thing." Torre said, "He throws hard."

If they were impressed, so was Ryan. "I'll tell you, that pitch Torre hit was one of the best balls I'd thrown all day," he later observed. "It was an up-and-in fastball, and he hit it to right field over the bullpen. That really impressed me because it showed you couldn't just throw in the big league to get by. You might overpower minor leaguers with a great fastball pitch, but not major leaguers. They'll wait for it and hit it. No matter how hard you throw it, if they know it's coming, they can connect with it.

"I still didn't have a curve or a change-up. I could throw a curve, but it wasn't a good one, and I couldn't get it over, and big leaguers will wait for a pitch that's over the plate. If the fast one's the only one you can get over, they'll wait for it and hit it. If you want to give them a walk, they'll take it. They won't chase bad pitches if you don't get them off-balance and behind in the count."

The Mets gave Nolan a start in Houston. Many of Ryan's family and friends from Refugio, Woodsboro, and Alvin attended, putting a lot of pressure on the youngster. Unused to big-city traffic, many got caught in traffic and arrived at the Astrodome late. Most of his family missed the first inning.

"It was a typical Nolan Ryan inning," Ryan recalls. "I walked a man, struck out a man, then walked another man. Somebody made a two-base error. Then they got a base hit. They got six runs. They got me out of there fast. By the time my people showed up in the second inning I was gone."

Embarrassed, Ryan brooded a bit. He did not get into another game. He got the loss in that game, and it was his only decision. In his three innings he had struck out six batters, but walked three and given up five hits and five runs, all earned. Translated into nine-inning terms, his ERA was a nifty 15.00.

Nevertheless, he'd seen the Met pitchers and hadn't seen anything awesome. No one had won more than 11 games on the staff, and only two had won more than they lost. Jack Fisher, Dennis Ribant, Bob Shaw, and Jack Hamilton were the starters, and they seldom finished what they started. Four regular pitchers had earned run averages above four runs a game, and two were above five runs a game.

With three teams in three leagues that season, Ryan had fanned 313 batters in 205 innings, and he had the sort of arm that represented the team's hope for the future. "I knew I couldn't do a lot yet, but I felt I could do more than some pitchers they had. I had hopes they would overlook my being beat up in my only start and look to me to make their staff the next season," he says.

He was wrong. Devine decided it would be foolish to push him forward too fast. Westrum says, "I wanted to try him, but the feeling was he wasn't ready, and they didn't want to risk his future by forcing him into the big leagues before he was ready. He was very rough."

Times were tough. Westrum was to be fired before the next season was finished as the Mets fell back to tenth and last place for the sixth time in seven seasons and lost more than 100 games once more. Meanwhile, Ryan encountered rough going all year.

He was called into reserve service duty before the season started. He had to put in Army time before he could even report back to pro ball, and he would have to put in part of each pro season in service every season for several seasons after that.

Returning from his service stint, Ryan was hurried through two weeks of spring training in Florida, tuned up with a four-inning pitching stint for Winter Haven in the Florida State League, then was sent to Jacksonville in the International League.

He struck out 5 in four shutout innings for Winter Haven, then 18 in seven innings at Jacksonville. But he also hurt his arm. "I hadn't thrown the ball while in basic training, and my arm was tight when I got out," he recalls. "I threw too hard too soon."

His feat of fanning 18 out of twenty-one outs at Jacksonville brought Bing Devine by air to Florida to take a close look. Ryan says, "The papers got wind Devine was coming down, and they started calling me the next Sandy Koufax. The night I was scheduled to pitch the ball park was packed. Six thousand and some people—the biggest crowd they'd ever had.

"Bill Virdon was the manager. Before the game I came up to him and said, 'My arm hurts.' And he said, 'Go out and warm up.' The first two warm-ups I threw I knew something was really wrong, so I went back to the dugout and said, 'I can't do it.' "The Jacksonville general manager was there, and he said, 'The hell you can't, son. Those are people out there, and they're going to want their money back if you don't pitch.' I said, 'Nope, I can't.'

"The general manager starts begging me, and I still said I couldn't. Then he wanted me to go out to home plate and announce that I couldn't pitch so they'd at least know I was on the team. But Bill Virdon said that was going too far. It turned out only two or three people demanded a refund anyway."

A doctor diagnosed Ryan's problem as a torn tendon in his forearm. It took a long time to heal, and his bosses by then had decided to practice patience with their prize. He did not pitch another inning all season. It was a lost season as far as he was concerned, with one exception. Nolan married his hometown sweetheart, Ruth Holdorff, on June 26, and waited for his future to unfold.

4   The Mets and the Majors

It was not clear that making the Mets and making the majors was the same thing.

When the Brooklyn Dodgers and New York Giants left for Los Angeles and San Francisco respectively, the 10,000,000 people in the metropolitan area of New York City were left without National League baseball in 1958. The next two largest cities retained two teams, but not the Big City. New Yorkers could not even see their former favorites as visitors and the natives grew restless.

This gap was supposed to be plugged by expansion, which created the New York Mets in 1962. Playing first in the old Polo Grounds until Shea Stadium was built, then in their spanking new playground on Long Island, the Mets did, indeed, bring in the Dodgers, Giants, and other attractive visitors, but they did not beat them very often, and it was not clear they really could be called a National League team.

Like other new teams, the Mets were stocked in a draft of the other teams' surplus players. These consisted of young players without much future, journeyman veterans, or old players with only a prideful past. Some new teams have luck with a few players. The Mets had no such luck. They were as bad as a big-league ball club could be.

The Mets were fortunate in only one way. The other team in town, the Yankees, had proven it was possible to win too much. The Bronx Bombers had dominated the American League and all baseball for so long that the thrill had gone out of it. They so seldom lost that it was boring when they won. Rooting for them was like rooting for U.S. Steel. There was no real competition or challenge.

The Mets arrived as the underdogs. They were funny, and it was fun to root for them. They so seldom won that it was a thrill when they did not lose. Every game, every play was a challenge. Their first year they drew more than 900,000 to the tenement in Harlem, while the Yankees drew 1,500,000 to their storied Stadium. The second year the Mets drew more than 1,000,000 fans, while the Yankees drew fewer than 1,300,000.

The Yankees had won their fourteenth pennant in seventeen seasons but had lost their grip on the public. All but their most ardent supporters were pleased when they began to slip. Meanwhile, the Mets with the worst team in baseball appealed to the fans. By their third year when they went into their new arena—Shea Stadium—the Mets pulled more than 1,700,000 and passed the Yankees in attendance.

The gap continued to grow. By 1966, when the

47

Yankees themselves had skidded into tenth place, they were struggling to top 1,000,000, while the Mets were approaching 2,000,000. The fans brought banners, rooted madly, and had a marvelous time. A typical banner read: YOU MAY BE DOWN ON YOUR CANS, BUT YOU'RE FIRST WITH YOUR FANS. In 1967 the Mets won 61 games, lost 101, and finished last, 50 full games out of first. But they drew more than 1,500,000. Still, this was a decline of almost 500,000 from the previous season.

When Nolan Ryan reported to the team's preseason camp in St. Petersburg, Florida, early in 1968, he arrived at a time when the fun of losing had faded with the fans and the Mets were aware they had to start to show promise or be dropped by the public. They had finished tenth five seasons out of six and as high as ninth only once. However, they had been rebuilt in this time, and there now was promise on the roster, though few realized it then.

Gil Hodges, a former Dodger star who had been popular in New York and had shown promise managing an expansion team in Washington, had been brought in to manage the Mets, and this stirred new interest. Young players signed in the early years had progressed through the minors and were ready for the majors, raising some high hopes.

The Mets had come up with a steady catcher, Jerry Grote; a slick shortstop, Bud Harrelson; and a trio of strong outfielders, Cleon Jones, Tommie Agee, and Ron Swoboda. They had little power, but plenty of pitching prospects. Such strong-armed, hard-throwing hurlers as Tom Seaver, Jerry Koosman, Tug McGraw,

Nolan Ryan, and Gary Gentry were their real reasons for a rise.

Seaver had won 16 games as a rookie in 1967 to establish himself, but the others were rookies in 1968, still trying to become established. Koosman and Mc-Graw made the club in the spring. Gentry did not. Ryan almost did not. He arrived on a wave of publicity touting him as the greatest thing since sliced bread. But his arm still was healing, he strained it further, trying to impress the brass too soon, and he was suffering from blisters which developed on his right index finger. Still, pitching coach Rube Walker touted him from the first time he saw him: "His fast has a heap of hurry on it," he said.

Johnny Murphy, the general manager of the Mets at the time, observed sourly, "He's got a great arm, but he can't pitch. He's always got some kind of ache or pain." Gil Hodges, the new manager, said, "I've heard what he can do, but I haven't seen it yet." Some of Ryan's teammates started to call him the Myth. The shy young man was withdrawn and lonely as he struggled to display his pitching talent.

Near the end of the exhibition trail Hodges gave Nolan a last chance against the St. Louis Cardinals. Ryan was worked for four innings, and he was ready. He struck out five of the first six batters he faced and blanked the Birds during his stint. "Well, I've seen it, and he is something else," said Hodges. "I have to keep him now."

Writer Paul Zimmerman observed, "The legend has come to life."

Ryan arrived in New York following a flood of newspaper stories hailing him as "another Bob Feller, a right-handed Sandy Koufax," and other such incredible comparisons he was not nearly ready to justify. Almost everyone was expecting more from him than he could yet give. "I had a lot of pressure on me," he remembers. "It shook me up. I was just a kid."

He was twenty-one years old and had only 170 pounds on his six-foot two-inch frame. He had rare ability, but he was neither physically nor mentally mature. Joe Durso of the New York *Times* recalls, "He was very shy, a humble kid. He didn't know how to handle the press, and there were a lot of writers and broadcasters coming at him all the time. He was nice to them but awed by them. On the mound he could throw hard, but he was unsure of himself. When he'd walk a guy, he'd sort of walk around with his head down. I mean, you hardly got the impression he was in charge out there."

Well, this was no tried and proven veteran ready to challenge the great hitters. He'd seen few major-league games, much less pitched in them. He had pitched in only two. He'd been a pro only a little more than two years. He had struck out 445 batters in 291 innings in the minors. He had pitched only eleven innings the year before. And he had been hurried into the majors.

The season started in San Francisco. The Mets as usual lost their opener. And in typical Met manner—on a wild relay throw home in the ninth inning. But the Mets won the next game on a shutout by Koosman in Los Angeles. The next night, the Mets were shut out by Don Drysdale in LA. They went to Houston. In the Mets' fourth game of the campaign, before friends and family, Ryan shut out the Astros for seven innings, and when his finger got sore, Danny Frisella finished off the shutout the last two innings.

The Mets won, 4–0, and Ryan got the victory. "It's a terrific thrill," he said, sweaty and tired, but excited, in the dressing room afterward. "I guess the first one is always a thrill. And here in Texas, with so many people pulling for me, it was an extra thrill. I was throwing well. I hope it's only the first of many." Hodges said, "If he throws like that, he'll win a lot. He was smoking."

The Mets lost the next day, 1–0, on an error in the infield in the twenty-fourth inning. Wearily, they returned to New York for the home opener. A turnout of 52,000 fans welcomed their heroes, and Koosman pitched another shutout to jar the Giants. The next day Willie Mays' three-run double beat the Mets. The next day Ryan struck out 11 Dodgers in less than seven innings before being relieved but lost, 3–2.

Through April, May, and June Nolan worked in the regular rotation, except when he had weekend reserve service duty. He pitched pretty well. He was not often hit hard. He was beaten in some close games but was a winner more often than he was a loser.

Early in May he struck out 10 and with relief help from Ron Taylor shut out the Phils, 3–0, on three hits at Shea. In his next start he stopped the Cardinals in St. Louis, 4–1. Back home, he fanned 14 and trimmed the Reds, 3–2. In San Francisco early in June he blanked the Giants with Cal Koonce's help, 4–0. In mid-month, he struck out 12 Astros but lost, 6–5, in ten innings.

The Mets were 28-29 in the middle of June, the closest they had been to .500 that late in their history, but they could not climb over the break-even mark and started to fall off after that, although they won more often than they had in the past. Seaver and Koosman carried the club, pitching tremendously well.

Ryan pitched well but rarely could finish what he started. He had to be bailed out after seven or eight innings when a blister would develop on the index finger of his pitching hand.

Met trainer Gus Mauch would lance, drain, and bandage the blister between starts and Ryan's finger would heal, but the next start a new blister would develop. In an effort to toughen the finger, Mauch resorted to an old home remedy, requiring Ryan to soak his hand in pickle brine purchased from a delicatessen in the Bronx near Yankee Stadium. Apparently it had better brine than those on Long Island near Shea Stadium. And it helped, but not enough. The blister still formed, sooner or later. And Ryan hated the remedy. "I hated the smell of the pickle brine. I smelled like a delicatessen," he said. A Texas boy, he was not used to the smell of a New York delicatessen. And Nolan's teammates teased him.

By the end of July Ryan had won 6 games and lost only 3. But he had started 18 and finished only 3. The blisters were bothering him a lot, and he was due to go to summer camp with the Army reserves for two weeks in August. The Mets had started to struggle, and Hodges was looking around for areas in which he could help his team. He conferred with General Manager Murphy, and they decided to put Ryan on the thirty-day disabled list, so they could summon another pitcher from the minors. Told he would be put out of action for a month, Ryan protested, but rookies do not win arguments from management.

"I'd been pitching pretty well despite the blisters, without complaint, and I said it would slow my development if I was sidelined that long," Ryan remembers. "However, they pointed out I would be sidelined for a while anyway because of my obligation to reserve duty, and this would give my finger a chance to heal. Actually, it wasn't about to heal. Not really. As soon as I started using it extensively again, the blisters would begin again. What I was really afraid of was losing my place in the starting rotation. I sure was right about that."

He never got it back. He was idled a month. When he returned on September 1, he was rusty. He was buried in the bullpen and never got out. Because he was wild, he wasn't an ideal reliever anyway. The ideal reliever throws hard, as Ryan did, but with control, which Ryan was without. And Ryan was wary of throwing hard and tight to batters. He wasn't tough. During his layoff, he had lost his rhythm. When he did pitch, he was pressing to prove himself all over again and was not relaxed. He did not do well and lost his last five decisions. He never got another start after July 29 and finished his season with 6 victories and 9 defeats. He struck out 133 batters in 134 innings and walked 75. His earned run average was respectable at 3.09.

It was a difficult time for him. He was not at home in New York. "It was the opposite of my small-town life in Texas," he says. "It was crowded. You had to park on the street and couldn't enjoy your yard. It was a very little yard. We had a house in Queens. Right

53

behind us was a big apartment building. It was congested, the whole area. We didn't even enjoy going shopping, conditions were so crowded. And the people weren't very friendly. It was a hectic place to live." Nolan and Ruth were homesick for Alvin.

He had complaints about the club. He says, "Hodges was a smart baseball man and a good man, but he was distant. Gil didn't talk to his players much. If you're a person having problems like I was, you want a boss you can communicate with." His pitching coach, Rube Walker, was effective in that he knew how to get a pitcher in shape, he knew how often he should work, and he knew how to set up hitters. But he'd been a catcher, and he just wasn't able to help a pitcher with fundamentals. He didn't pick up Nolan's mistakes, and Nolan didn't learn much.

"I wasn't a big-league pitcher," he recalls. "I should have been down in Double A learning how to pitch. If you saw Nolan Ryan pitch against a Juan Marichal or a Bob Gibson, you knew it was pitiful. Because of my ability to throw hard, I could get by as long as I worked regularly, but I only had one way to win, I only had one pitch, and I didn't have anything extra for emergencies. When I got into a jam, I didn't know how to get out of it. I really wasn't ready. And once I was sidelined the month I really lost my touch, I really started to struggle.

"After a while the team was losing a lot, and the attitude on the team was bad. They'd been losing so long they expected to lose. When they got off to a pretty good start and won some games, they started to gain confidence, but they lost it when they started to lose again. By the time I was restored to the roster everyone just wanted the last month to end, so the season would end, and no one had much enthusiasm. It's a difficult thing to go through, especially a young guy who goes in with such high hopes."

The high hopes for the Mets ended in ninth place, but at least it wasn't tenth and last. With 73 victories and 89 defeats, they finished 24 games from first. But this was a big improvement over past performances. The Mets were almost ready, even if Ryan wasn't.

5   To the Heights, Briefly

The Mets made a mistake. All teams make mistakes, but none ever made one bigger than the one the Mets made about Nolan Ryan. Near the end of spring training in 1969 he was pitching against the Pirates in an exhibition game and was hit on the elbow by a line drive. It hurt terribly. He couldn't pitch powerfully, so he was sent to the bullpen at the start of the season. He worked irregularly and erratically the first month of the season. The Mets began to think about trading him. They didn't do so right away, but they did eventually. Other teams made mistakes by not grabbing him before one finally did.

The Mets had top pitching. Seaver had won 16 games and Koosman 19 in 1968. Seaver would win 25 and Koosman 17, while Gentry would arrive with 13 in 1969. But the Mets lacked punch. They looked around and discovered that Atlanta was willing to part with Joe Torre, a slugging catcher and first baseman in return for pitching and depth. Torre was a Brooklyn boy, and the Mets figured he would be popular, as well as productive for them.

The Braves asked for Ryan, Jerry Grote, and Amos Otis in return for Torre. Paul Richards, the executive director in Atlanta, always was sharp on pitchers and admitted later it was Ryan he wanted. "I figured he just needed time to develop into a powerful pitcher," Richards said. The Mets weren't willing to wait. They knew Nolan could throw hard, but they didn't think he was strong and doubted he would develop. They wanted a winner right away. But they balked at the trade because they didn't want to part with Otis, who had talent.

The Mets countered with an offer of J. C. Martin, Ed Kranepool, Ryan or Jim McAndrew, and a minor leaguer in return for Torre and Bob Aspromonte, another Brooklyn boy. They seemed more interested in getting Brooklyn boys than the best ballplayers. As for Ryan or McAndrew, they didn't care which. McAndrew was the pitcher they had called up when they sidelined Ryan in 1968. McAndrew was winning four and losing seven, while Ryan was denied an opportunity to develop. In the next five years McAndrew only once won more games than he lost and never won as many as a dozen games in any single year.

The Braves rejected the deal, and it died. The Mets later made a deal for Donn Clendenon, a veteran first baseman who could hit the long ball, and he did help them when they needed help.

Listed as 100–1 longshots in the odds out of Las Vegas as the season started, the Mets lost 14 of their first 23 games and were in last place early in May, when

Ryan got his first start. The league had been divided into two divisions, and the Mets were last in the East when they went into Chicago. Ryan was whipping the Cubs, 2–1, when he pulled a groin muscle and had to leave the game. He was sent back to the bullpen to recuperate. Two weeks later Houston was in New York, and the Astros loaded the bases when Ryan was brought in to relieve. He retired Jesus Alou on three pitches but pulled the groin muscle again and was put back on the disabled list.

He did not return to active duty until late June. He fanned 10 Phils, but lost, 6–5, in ten innings. In July Army duty was beckoning, the blisters were bothering him again, and his groin muscle remained tender. By the time he got back from his reserve stint he was rusty and out of rhythm. He was buried back in the bullpen, summoned for only an occasional start in spots when Hodges was short of pitchers. The Mets by then had moved into the pennant race and were not willing to risk a raw talent like Ryan's to start critical games.

Manager Leo Durocher's Chicago Cubs had taken off on a tremendous start and had the Windy City howling in hope of a pennant. They won 9 of their first 10 games and 49 of their first 76 and put Pittsburgh and St. Louis away early. But then they started to slow down. Maybe they thought they had it won. Once they lost their momentum they couldn't get rolling again. The Mets won 11 straight and slipped into second place, but it was still hard to take them seriously.

The Mets moved to within 5 games of first during the Fourth of July weekend, the traditional midpoint in the season. The Cubs came to town for a critical series. They led, 3–1, in the ninth inning of the opener, but young center fielder Don Young misplayed two balls, and the Mets won, 4–3. A disappointed Durocher publicly rapped the lad. So did Cub captain Santo. It seemed to destroy the Cubs as a team. It created a division between the players and the manager. With harmony lost, they began to come apart and couldn't get together again.

The only base runner they got against Seaver the next game was on a single by rookie Jim Qualls with one out in the ninth inning. The Mets won, 4–0, to rise within 3 of the top. The Cubs salvaged the finale, but they were a troubled team now.

The Mets went into Chicago and took two out of three to continue closing in. From mid-July into August the Mets started to feel the pressure and lost 13 out of 23 games, but the Cubs were scrambling and could gain only 6 games. The first week in August the Mets had fallen 9½ back, but the Cubs weren't winning often anymore. Once the Mets started to win again the Cubs came right back to them.

The Cubs lost 8 out of 10, while the Mets won 12 out of 13 to surge to within 2½ games of the top as the teams turned into September. The Cubs came to town, and the Mets swept two straight as consecutive capacity crowds of close to 60,000 each roared their surprised satisfaction. A little improvement had pulled Met attendance to above 1,700,000 in 1968, and a pennant pushed it to better than 2,100,000 in 1969.

The Mets moved into first place the next day, September 10, and all around the Mets was madness. They went in front in a doubleheader with Montreal, winning the first game, 3–2, in the twelfth inning and winning the second game, 7–1, behind Ryan's 11-strikeout stuff. It was one of his few good opportunities during the entire season and he came through in high style.

The Mets continued to pull away, playing to pennant-crazed crowds at home and surprised, sympathetic spectators on the road. They were the talk of the sporting world.

The Mets won 44 games and lost only 19 the last two months of the season, while the Cubs won 28 games and lost 29. The Mets came from 9½ games back to top the Cubs by 8. Whereas they were used to losing 100 games a season, they won 100 and lost only 62 this season, soaring from ninth to first in one season in one of the greatest upsets in sports history.

The actual pennant clincher came in their last home game of the season, Wednesday night, September 24, as a cheering crowd of more than 56,000 fans saw Donn Clendenon clout two home runs off Super Steve Carlton. Gentry pitched a four-hitter for a 6–0 triumph that set off a celebration that spread clear across the country.

Champagne was poured in the delirious dressing room scene, but Nolan Ryan stood off to the side almost as though he were a stranger. He smiled wistfully. "It was tremendously exciting, and I've been excited by it, and I'm pleased as heck for the guys, but I don't feel all that much a part of it, I didn't get to give that much to it."

He had pitched in only 25 games, most in brief relief. He had started only 10 games and finished only 2. He had won only 6 and lost only 3. He had pitched only 89 innings the whole long season, striking out 92 and walking 47. That worked out to a strikeout an inning, but also about five walks a nine-inning game. His earned run average was only ordinary at 3.54.

"He's not a polished pitcher, he was hurt a lot, and we just couldn't take a chance on him," Hodges observed.

"I just didn't get much chance to help the team," Ryan observed.

Curiously, the postseason play-offs and World Series proved a little different.

Almost everyone expected the Met bubble to burst in postseason play. The assumption was that they had been playing over their heads, would have spent themselves in the pennant push, and would come back down to earth in championship contests that for them would be almost anticlimactic.

Almost everyone was wrong.

The first National League play-offs opened in Atlanta, where the Braves had bombed their way to the divisional laurels in the West behind the bats of such sluggers as Henry Aaron, Rico Carty, and Orlando Cepeda. The Braves were heavy favorites to win the best-of-five series.

The Mets won the opener, 9–5, and the Braves were disgusted with themselves.

The Braves let the Mets build a 9–1 lead in the second game before they started to pull themselves together. They KO'd Koosman and pulled to within 9–6 before the Mets pulled away again to win, 11–6.

The Mets went to New York needing only one victory to win the series but aware that if the Braves began to bounce back, the Met bubble might burst.

Some 53,000 frenzied fans flowed into the cement saucer on Monday in hopes of hollering their heroes home before the game and maybe the Series got away from them.

Gentry started but got only one out before Aaron's two-run homer put him and the Mets behind. He got through the second inning but got in trouble again in the third. Gonzales slashed a single to open the inning. Aaron drove a double to left-center to put two men in scoring position.

Behind, 2–0, with two on and none out and Carty coming up, the Mets were in hot water with the pivotal contest seemingly about to be settled early. Hodges got Ryan and other relievers up to warm up hurriedly in the bullpen but let Gentry pitch to Carty.

Gentry got a strike and a ball on Carty. His next pitch was ripped by Rico down the left-field line toward the seats. For a split second it looked like a three-run homer that would put the big game beyond reach. But then it curved just foul. The Mets and their fans heaved a big sigh of relief.

Hodges made his move. Surprisingly, he summoned Ryan in to relieve right then. Managers seldom call in relievers in the middle of a batter's turn. The count was one ball and two strikes, but the starter was being shelled, and Carty's "foul homer" hurried Hodges' decision. No one expected it to be the wild, inexperienced, underworked Ryan. "I didn't expect it myself," Nolan admitted later. "But it was a chance to contribute to the club, a chance to do well, and I was determined."

The tension was tremendous as the twenty-two-year-old warmed up. Ready, he took his sign as Carty set himself. Ryan reared back, strode forward and hurled a blur right across the plate. "I didn't see it till it was past me," Carty confessed later. It stunned him. He never even swung. The umpire's right thumb shot skyward. He shouted, "Strike three!" The fans came up yelling.

Ryan bent back to business. With first base open, Hodges ordered an intentional walk to Cepeda, loading the bases to set up a force-out at any base for the second out or a double play for the third out. It wasn't needed. Clete Boyer, who'd had a big year with the bat, came up and went down on strikes, the third one called. Ryan threw three blurred streaks, and Boyer later said, "I've never seen a man throw a faster pitch. The third one was so fast I couldn't get my bat off my shoulder."

Bo Didier got his bat off his shoulder but got only a small piece of the underside of a Ryan delivery and popped it in the air to left, where Jones caught it for the third out. The fans sent young Nolan Ryan off to a standing ovation. He was happy, and he tipped his cap in appreciation. It had been tremendous relief pitching, coming in with two on and none out, being forced to put a third man on to load the bases, but getting three outs without a run scoring.

The game still had to be won, however.

Agee hit a homer in the home half to cut the Met deficit in half.

Ryan got Cesar Garrido on a fly ball, Pat Jarvis on a strikeout, and Felix Millan on a grounder for a one, two, three fourth. Shamsky singled and Boswell homered in the home half to put the Mets ahead, 3–2.

In the first of the fifth Ryan got Gonzalez on a groundout and Aaron on a pop-up. With two out, he may have let down a little. He went to three and two on Carty, then missed and walked him. Nolan got two strikes on Cepeda, saw him foul off two more strikes, then got one too good to him, and the big guy hit it over the fence in left-center for two runs, and the Braves were ahead, 4–3.

Hodges stayed with Ryan, and Nolan got Boyer on a fly ball to finish off the threat. The young pitcher did not make any more mistakes.

Upset with himself, he went to the plate hungrily in the home half to lead off and bounced a single through the right side. He'd had only three hits all season. After Agee flied out, Garrett ripped a home run to right to put the Mets ahead again, 5–4. Jones doubled, and Jarvis was pulled. But Boswell's single off reliever George Stone made it 6–4.

In the seventh Ryan got Millan on a fly to left, fanned Gonzalez with blazers, and bore down to get the amazing Aaron on a pop-up for the second straight time.

Opening the eighth, Carty was fooled by a pitch and topped it but beat out a slow roller. Ryan bore down with blazers. He got called third strikes past Cepeda and Boyer. "He was humming that thing," said an awed Boyer. "Coming up, it looked as small as an aspirin tablet and blurry. I knew it was past me when I heard it smack into the catcher's glove. The catcher's hands must have been sore for a week."

Lum pinch-hit for Didier and singled to left, Carty stopping at second. Felipe Alou pinch-hit with two on and two out and hit the ball on a line to Harrelson at short, and Ryan had escaped again.

He singled in the last half. "I was high as a kite," he said later. But there were two out, and Agee went out to end the threat. Ryan had to go out to work the ninth to protect his team's lead with three outs to go to the pennant.

Hodges and Walker talked to Ryan to make sure he felt fine. He said he felt fine. This was the seventh inning he was working, but he felt strong, and his finger felt fine. Catcher Grote cautioned him not to try to strike out the side, but to get the ball over with something on it and let the fielders do the work.

Aspromonte pinch-hit and hit a soft fly to center, caught by Agee. One out. Millan hit and bounced a grounder to Harrelson at short, and Bud threw to first to retire him. Two out. The fans were roaring on every pitch now. Gonzalez was overpowered by a hard one, got his bat on it, but bounced it to Garrett at third, who fired to first. Three out.

As their fans stood and cheered, the Mets poured all over the triumphant relief pitcher to hail their hero of the day. The Mets had won the pennant play-off and were on their way to the World Series. Amid the tumult in their quarters later Ryan, flushed and damp, grinned broadly and said, "This has to be the greatest game of my life. I got a chance to give something to this team. I'm only happy I could help them win the big game."

It was the biggest game in their history at that time. Ryan had pitched three-hit two-run ball, striking out seven and walking only two, one intentionally, in seven innings under pounding pressure against some of the best batters in baseball.

He had come through in the clutch and for the first time in his two major-league seasons had scaled the summit of stardom. Reporters and broadcasters surrounded him and pressed him for the secret of his success. He held up well. "Was I scared? I sure was." He smiled. "Did I feel the pressure? Yes. Well, I just pitched as best I could. Yes, this is about the best I have pitched. But I feel I can pitch. I hope I'll get more chances to pitch now."

The World Series opened in Baltimore. The Orioles were heavily favored to win the best-of-seven set. They had won what would be the first of three straight American League pennants. They had a balanced ball club with such heavy hitters as Frank Robinson, Brooks Robinson, and Boog Powell, fine fielders, and dependable pitchers such as Dave McNally, Jim Palmer, and Mike Cuellar.

The first game was the second Saturday in October. Don Buford hit the first pitch from Seaver into the seats for the first run. Seaver wasn't sharp, fell behind, 4–0, and was beaten, 4–1. Cuellar confined the Mets. So everyone supposed that was the beginning of the end for the "Amazing Mets."

But Koosman carried a no-hitter into the seventh inning of the second game and wound up winning with help from reliever Ron Taylor. It was won, 2–1, from McNally on three ground-ball singles after two were out for a run in the ninth. It was as though the fates were on the side of the Mets.

The teams moved to New York for the third game Tuesday. It was cloudy and cool, and the crowd of more than 56,000 fans filled Shea Stadium with noise.

While Ryan remained in the bullpen, unused so far, the rookie Gentry got the start against Palmer. Agee greeted Palmer with a home run. In the second, Gentry himself doubled in two runs. Grote doubled in another in the sixth to make it 4–0.

Gentry started to struggle in the fourth. He got out of a two-on, two-out jam when Agee crashed into the fence to catch a smash by Elrod Hendricks.

But in the seventh Gentry, who had worked out of a jam in the sixth, got into another. Hendricks hammered a deep fly to center, which Agee ran back to catch. Dave Johnson drove another deep fly to center, and again Agee got back in the deepest part of the ball park to catch it.

Shaken, the rookie went wild and walked Belanger, May, and Buford to fill the bases. Belatedly, Hodges summoned a reliever, Ryan. Nolan, working for only the second time in two weeks, pitched two fastballs past Paul Blair and another fastball which Blair managed to swing at. He had only a hunk of it, and the ball spun off his bat, curving toward right-center. It might have fallen in, but Agee reached for it on the run, slid on one knee, and caught it inches above the ground.

Ryan walked off in relief as the crowd applauded Agee.

In the eighth Frank Robinson flied to Agee at the center-field fence. Ryan, finding his rhythm, ripped fastballs plateward. Powell watched a third strike blaze past. "It was too hot to touch," he said, laughing ruefully later. Brooks Robinson worked Ryan to a three-and-two count, then ripped at a fastball, and missed it for strike three. "It's hard to hit what you can't see," he said later.

In the home half Kranepool hit a home run to make it 5–0.

Ryan could coast in the ninth. He was working easy. Maybe too easy. He may have been overconfident. He got Hendricks and Johnson on fly balls. He went to a full count on Belanger, missed, and walked him. He went to work on Clay Dalrymple, who hit to second on a line. Weis knocked the ball down but couldn't make a play. Ryan then worked so carefully on Buford he walked him, filling the bases.

After a conference on the mound Nolan was permitted to continue. The dangerous Blair batted. Ryan pitched with all his power. The ball sailed as it sizzled plateward. He got two strikes on Blair, then threw one past him so hard the batter never swung at it. As the umpire shouted the third strike for the third out, reliever Ryan was mobbed again as the fans cheered.

The Mets had won, with Ryan wrapping up the shutout in a tense situation. "I want to thank Tommie Agee," Ryan said later. But Ryan was good, too. "I was good. I was good and strong. Maybe too strong. I was wild. But it was a big win and I'm happy to have helped," he said.

Incredibly, he would not get another chance to help that Series. He had pitched 2-1/3 innings of one-hit shutout ball, walking two and striking out three, and it was the last time he would get a call in 1969.

Seaver pitched ten innings to win the fourth game, 2–1, to give the Mets a three games to one lead in the Series.

After Clendenon's homer Seaver nursed a 1–0 lead into the ninth. Two hits and a near hit tied the game, but Swoboda's diving catch on Brooks Robinson's liner to right-center saved it.

The Orioles let Grote's little fly fall safely in short left in the tenth for two bases. Gaspar ran for him. Martin bunted to pitcher Pete Richert, whose throw to first hit the runner's wrist and ricocheted away. Gaspar ran home with the winner.

In the sixth game pitcher McNally hit a homer off Koosman in the second to help carry the Orioles to a 3–0 lead. But the Mets truly were amazing. This was their year. Whatever they tried worked. In the sixth Jones was hit in the foot by a pitch. Clendenon hit a homer, and the deficit had been cut to 3–2. In the seventh little Al Weis, who had hit only two homers during the regular season, hit one, and there was no longer a deficit.

In the eighth Jones doubled, and Swoboda doubled him home. The fans went wild. The Mets led, 4–3, and their players hollered happily from the dugout, while Ryan and other relievers watched happily from the bullpen. In the eighth the Mets scratched out another run to make it 5–3. Entering the ninth, they needed three outs to win the World Series, most unbelievably. In the ball park and in front of TV sets, stunned fans watched with excitement.

Frank Robinson walked. Boog Powell hit a grounder to Weis, who forced the runner at second. Brooks Robinson flied to Swoboda in right. Johnson flied to Jones in left. As Cleon caught it, the Mets were champs, their fans exploded, and Koosman came off the mound to be "buried" by his delighted teammates.

The dressing room was wild with the celebration of the champions. Ryan was one, if not a key one. He was, as usual, subdued, not one of the wild ones. "This is super," he said as he watched the winners whooping and hollering. He'd played an important part in it, if not the most important part.

The celebration was carried on throughout New York the next day as the Mets were treated to a ticker-tape parade through downtown streets lined with joyous citizens. In the following days, weeks, and months, the Amazing Mets were the toast of the sporting world. They were interviewed endlessly, invited onto television, buried under book bids. Not much of this business was brought to Ryan, a fringe performer for the champs.

Scene: In the Met clubhouse six of the team's pitchers line up in uniform in front of manager Gil Hodges. He picks up a piece of paper and says, "Now listen to me, you guys: The commissioner has given a direct order. Anyone suspected of using grease on his hair for purposes of throwing a grease ball shall be immediately removed from the game. Everybody hear that?"

Tom Seaver, Jerry Koosman, Don Cardwell, Cal Koonce, Nolan Ryan, and Gary Gentry nod. Hodges goes down the line, inspecting each pitcher's hair. When he gets to Gentry, he notices he is nervous. Hodges walks behind him and lifts his cap and rubs his hair. "Grease," says the manager solemnly. "Gentry, you're the first pitcher ever sent to the showers without throwing a ball."

Gentry turns and walks sadly toward the shower room. As he does, Hodges throws him a bottle of "greaseless Vitalis." The commercial which has been taped will be shown all over the country on television.

A Rheingold beer commercial says, in part, "They

come from places like Van Meter, Iowa, and Alvin, Texas, with arms that fire bullets. . . ."

No names are used. Bob Feller apparently is the only pitcher ever to arrive from Van Meter. And his bullet-throwing "successor," Nolan Ryan, the only one out of Alvin.

"Alvin is so small it doesn't even have a last name," says Jerry Koosman.

Nolan Ryan laughs. He got a little extra money for the Vitalis nonspeaking appearance, but none for the nameless mention in the Rheingold commercial.

Today almost all athletes need managerial help. Nolan Ryan uses the services of Mattgo Enterprises, a respected New York operation run by Matt Merola and Paul Goetz. In 1969, however, Seaver, Koosman, and Gentry were more highly regarded and better known than Nolan, despite Nolan's heroics in one play-off and one World Series game.

Maybe the Mets did not make many mistakes in pulling a pennant out of a hat that season, but they were making one on Nolan by not permitting him to develop to his potential. They would win another pennant in a few seasons, but they wasted a pitcher who might have won them many pennants.

He did, as did each of his teammates, pick up a check for $18,338 as his share of his team's championship success, and it almost matched his $20,000 seasonal salary of that time.

He invested some of his money in his schooling, attending Alvin Junior College in pursuit of an education in veterinary medicine, which might provide him an occupation if pitching didn't.

Hurrying home after the World Series, he was worried about starting the fall semester late, having missed several weeks in biology and other classes because of his team's postseason play.

Aside from his studies, he also looked forward to tramping through the woods and hunting quail back home in Texas. He was trying to build himself up, hoping to earn a regular turn the following season.

Ryan had gained 20 pounds his first year in the majors and another 20 pounds his second year. Beefed up with 190 pounds on his six-two frame, he was maturing physically and believed he could become a key man for the defending champions.

However, he was doomed to have his ability wasted away. He'd hit the heights, briefly, but now would drop to the depths of disappointment.

6 Down to the Depths

It is a Tuesday night in New York in mid-July.
Despite daylong drizzle and black rain clouds overhead, a crowd of 35,000 fans has turned out at Shea
Stadium to see the world champion Mets entertain the
Cincinnati Reds. It is Nolan Ryan's regular turn in the
starting rotation, and many of the fans have turned out
to see the fastballer face the mighty "Big Red Ma-
chine." But Ryan is not pitching. He has been buried
back in the bullpen. Jim McAndrew is pitching, and
Ryan is brooding back in the bullpen. He wonders why
as he sits far from the field while jets from nearby La
Guardia Airport thunder overhead.

McAndrew never will amount to much. Ryan will.
It is as though everyone saw this except the Met management. Manager Gil Hodges is saying down in the
clubhouse, "His reserve meetings, the blisters on his
fingers, the fact that he hasn't pitched that much baseball and has a tendency to be inconsistent—these things

have held him back. Nolan *is* a hard worker, conscientious. He's made big strides this year toward more poise and maturity. He's got more confidence and control than ever before. . . ."

His voice drifts off. If he's coming along so well, why, then, isn't he getting more opportunity to develop?

Hodges smiles wearily and says, "Well . . . the idea is to win, and you can't build the individual up at the expense of that idea, no matter how much talent he's got."

Pitching coach Rube Walker says, "The first thing you think of with Nolan is that great arm. You close your eyes and see that arm and think how great he can be."

But he's not great yet?

"No," Walker says, sadly. "Nolan needs more concentration. He will get wild in the strike zone, which is as bad as being wild out of the strike zone and walking hitters. He's got to think when he's throwing that ball. As fast as Nolan is, if he gives the batter two, three good chances in the strike zone to hit, the chances are that's just what the batter will do."

So they were just not willing to take many chances on him.

What did his teammates think?

Pitcher Jerry Koosman, sitting in the dressing room autographing a boxful of baseballs for later distribution, said, "Nolan and I played together in Triple A ball down in Jacksonville in '67. All he had then was a fastball. He threw the thing so hard it didn't have time to curve. He's just born to throw that fastball.

"The day Tom Seaver struck out ten in a row, he was throwing as hard as Nolan does. There's been a night or two when I've thrown that hard, too. But Tom and I have to have everything going for us—our rhythm, our timing, our coordination—to throw as hard every once in a while as Nolan does consistently. And when Nolan has everything going for him, he throws just that much harder yet.

"He just needs a little more experience to get his control," Koosman concluded.

Pitcher Tug McGraw said, "I wish I had Nolan's potential. His problem is getting to know himself and learning how to put the ball where he wants to. When he was in the minors, he should have been getting that knowledge, but he was held back by the military duty and arm troubles. So now he's in the big leagues, and he doesn't have the solid minor-league background to go with it. He just needs to go out there and pitch more. He'll be all right," concluded McGraw.

Catcher Jerry Grote suggested, "Maybe Nolan's problem is he has too much stuff. He's just about the only guy I've seen who never gets any strikes called at the knee. The reason is that when his fastball is knee-high, it leaves his hand so low that the umpire can't believe it can rise up high enough to be a strike."

What did rivals say?

Chicago Cub slugger Ron Santo said, "Ryan is the hardest throwing right-hander I've ever faced. I think Koufax, who was left-handed, threw as hard as Ryan and was more effective because Koufax could get the ball over more consistently. It Ryan gains control he'll be a legend. Ryan has to let up on his fastball once in a while to get it over."

"Maybe," said hard-hitting second baseman Glenn Beckert, "but Ryan sure throws a lot harder than Wilbur Wood. I have to agree with Ron that Ryan is the hardest throwing right-hander I've seen."

Johnny Bench, the big hitter with the Cincinnati Reds, said, "I think the hitters are kidding themselves when they think anyone, right or left, throws as hard as Ryan. Maybe Koufax did. Maybe Gibson. They were great. Maybe great pitchers of the past like Bob Feller or Walter Johnson, who we never saw. But I don't see how anyone could throw faster than Ryan. I've never seen one who could. A Seaver or a Carlton can come close from time to time, but Ryan is fast all the time. I don't know anyone else who can bring that big fastball nine innings, game after game."

Cub pitching coach Larry Jansen, a fine pitcher in his younger days, said, "No one could throw harder, but in the big leagues you need something else to get by game after game. All he needs to do is to work in regular rotation, and he'll develop fast. He needs a curve he can get over once in a while to keep the hitters guessing. He has the potential to be one of the great ones," the coach concluded.

But Ryan wasn't working regularly in rotation, even though he had given the Mets some great games that season of 1970.

On April 18 Philadelphia came to town, and he shut them out on one hit and 15 strikeouts, 7–0. The only hit came in the first inning when leadoff man Denny Doyle singled. The Phils couldn't touch him the rest of the way.

Then, one week later, when the Mets were in Los Angeles, they did not get Ryan a single run, and he lost to Claude Osteen, 1–0, although he allowed only two hits.

In San Francisco, five days later, Nolan three-hit the Giants, winning 4–1.

By the end of April he appeared to be approaching his peak.

Then, swiftly, he slipped from it. He was wild and was hit hard in several starts. Late in May Chicago came to New York, and Nolan stopped the Cubs, 3–1. Then Houston came in, and he beat them, 4–3. Then he was roughed up again a couple of times.

Now it was the middle of June, and he was being passed over in turn supposedly because he was due to report for a weekend of Army duty. But he was not due to report for three days.

That day the twenty-three-year-old Ryan sat in his apartment and glumly recounted his season, which, following his super performances under pressure in the 1969 play-offs and World Series, should have been a big one.

"I thought 1970 was going to be my year," he observed wistfully. "My legs were in great shape from hunting in the winter, my arm was strong, my curve and change of pace were coming along, I was learning how to work the hitters better, and I finally solved the blister problem.

"Instead of soaking the finger in pickle brine, I take a scalpel and cut the callus back until it gets pink. I leave it almost raw and ready to bleed. It gets good and sore when I pitch, but there's no skin left to blister.

"So I'm ready to go, but I don't get the call. Instead of starting in the rotation, I'm put in the bullpen, and I'm not even called in for relief. The staff doesn't turn in a complete game for seven games, but I don't get a start.

"The thing is, Hodges feels that because I have to go to summer camp, I can't be in the rotation all year long. Because I have to go to Houston for a weekend meeting once a month, I can't always take my normal turn.

"I'm ready to pitch during the week when I have weekend meetings and on weekends when I'm in camp all week and ready to throw the day before and the day after reserve meetings, but for some reason that keeps him from thinking of me as a regular starter.

"I can go twelve days without throwing, and that can ruin your timing. So, finally, I got upset about it and went in to talk to him. So then I got a start against Philly.

"Back from before the end of the preseason exhibition games, I hadn't pitched for eighteen days. I told Ruth, 'My God, I feel like I'm pitching a World Series game,' it meant so much. Because if I have a good outing, I'm going back in the rotation. If not, back to the bullpen.

"Well, I give up a single to the leadoff hitter and that was it. A one-hitter. And I struck out fifteen guys. I got fourteen of them in the first six innings and had a shot at the one-game record, but I only got one more the rest of the game. But I pitched well."

He was asked what Hodges said then.

Ruth threw in the answer. "Nothing," she said, laughing a little at the wonder of it all.

Nolan laughed, too.

"Then we go to LA, and I lose a two-hitter, and on to San Francisco, where I win a three-hitter," he resumed. "It's looking good. I'm back in the rotation.

Hodges is showing confidence in me, doesn't get the bullpen throwing when I get in trouble.

"Then, suddenly, I'm back in trouble again. I have some wild outings. We're playing the Giants, and I feel I have great stuff warming up. The game starts. I throw a few fastballs, and they don't look right. So I call my catcher, Duffy Dyer, to the mound and say, 'How's my fastball?' He shakes his head and says, 'Nothing.' The Giants bomb me. There's no rhyme or reason to the way I pitch.

"I beat the Cubs on a two-hitter, and I'm getting stronger at the end of the game, just throwing it right past them. I strike out eleven guys in five innings against Houston and then run out of gas. You can't analyze it, it's so unpredictable." He was confused, frustrated, suffering for a regular opportunity to become the pitcher his one-hitter, his two-hitter, his three-hitter, and his strikeouts show he can be.

Later in the month he stifled the Cubs in Chicago, 6–1. But he spent part of July in camp and part of it back in the bullpen. He got only one decision all month, and that was a loss in San Diego. But he struck out 16 Padres in one thrilling game. Early in August he shut out the Cubs in Chicago, but then he was bombed in Pittsburgh and Atlanta and back in bad with his boss.

As the season wore on, his opportunities came fewer and farther between. The Mets struggled throughout the season, unable to make any more miracles. They had become a good team, but they were not the best. Following their championship campaign, advance sales for the season soared and interest in the team in the big town peaked. Attendance would reach nearly

2,700,000, a near-record turnout, and the people were disappointed by the Mets' performance.

Hodges was under horrible pressure. He had recovered from a severe heart attack and insisted he was all right when he took his team to the title the year before, but now many close to him had begun to worry about him. He kept saying, "All we need is a little winning streak to get going." But it never came, and the team never got going.

The team was close to the top most of the season, but didn't support its pitchers and couldn't come through in the clutch. Near the end of the season they lost three out of four games in a crucial series with Pittsburgh in New York and stranded twenty-nine runners.

The following weekend, the last weekend of the season, they remained in the running until they lost three straight in Pittsburgh, stranding thirty-two runners. Pittsburgh clinched the Eastern Division flag.

The Pirates won the pennant with only 89 victories. Clearly, they could have been beaten out. But the Cubs captured only 84 games to finish five games out. And the Mets won only 83 games to finish third, 6 games back. They lost 79.

Ryan won 7 games and lost 11. He started only 19 and finished only five. He was called on only eight times in relief. He worked only 132 innings, striking out 125. He also walked 97 batters, hit 4 and threw 8 wild pitches. His earned run average was an ordinary 3.41.

By season's end he was being used so seldom he was beginning to be bitter. "I wasn't getting to throw much, and by the time the season was over I was just glad to go home. I was frustrated and disappointed.

"I gave serious thoughts to retiring," he reveals. "I know I was young, but I felt I wasn't getting anywhere and wasn't getting the opportunity to get anywhere.

"I'd had some outstanding games and shown enough potential to be pitched in turn and permitted to develop, but all it took was a few bad pitches and I was being yanked for a reliever or a few bad games and I was being yanked from the rotation.

"The manager and the coaches seldom talked to me, much less helped me. It was like I'd be forgotten a week or two at a time. I began to wonder if there was any point to pursuing something that didn't seem to be there for me.

"If I'd had another source of income at the time, I would have quit," he confesses.

"I know I was young. Maybe I was too impatient. I know I wasn't a finished pitcher. But I didn't know how I'd ever get the polish I needed the way I was being used. I was starting to lose my confidence. I thought maybe it was time to get into something else in which I might make a future."

He thought about it through the winter. But by then he wanted to be the baseball pitcher he felt he could be. The money wasn't bad, and he and his wife wanted to have a family, so they decided he should go on with it for a time.

"I decided to give it at least one more year," he said.

But 1971 turned out to be another difficult year for the Mets and Ryan. Vida Blue became the hot young pitcher in baseball. Ryan stagnated. Before the season was over, he made it clear he wanted to be traded or he really might retire.

In 1970 Koosman struggled with arm miseries all

season, but the Mets never gave up on him and kept going back to him. Gentry was erratic and won only 9 games, but the club never gave up on him. Seaver won only 4 of his last 16 starts as the team tumbled from the race, but the club kept starting him.

In 1971 Koosman won only 6 games and lost 11, and Gentry was little better than a .500 pitcher, while Seaver slumped when the Mets went into a slump; but the club stuck with them. Eventually, Seaver rewarded the team's faith in him, even if the others did not, but the club gave up on Nolan Ryan.

At first, the twenty-four-year-old Ryan started regularly and responded spectacularly. He was 8–4 by the end of June. He had blanked the Cards in St. Louis, 7–0, won in San Diego, 2–1, and in Montreal, 4–1. At home, he blanked Pittsburgh, 4–0, beat Chicago, 2–1, beat Houston, 8–1, beat Atlanta, 6–2. But he seldom was permitted to finish a game. The minute he got into any trouble he was yanked.

He didn't get much help. He lost a 3–0 game in Los Angeles, a 2–0 game to the Dodgers in New York, and a 4–2 game to San Diego in New York.

He was disappointed, lost confidence, and started to press. Early in July he lost a 2–1 game to Montreal at Shea Stadium and wound up not winning a game all month. By then the Mets were out of the race. He won only one game in August, but the Mets were shut out in two of his losses in which he worked well. He suffered through September, winning only one more game.

The Mets were in contention at the outset, led the division by mid-May, still led after ten days of June, but then started to slip. They lost 11 out of 12 the first part of July while Pittsburgh was pouring it on. At that time, the Mets fell 10 games behind the Pirates and never got within 10 games of them the rest of the way. Pittsburgh won 97 games and lost 65. St. Louis won 90 and lost 72. The Mets and Cubs won 83 and lost 79 each to tie for third place, 14 games back of the winners.

More than 2,200,000 disappointed people paid their way into Shea Stadium, putting more pressure on Hodges, whose health faded. He would not live to see another season. The team's attitude went bad during the bad days, and they were fading at the finish, frustrated and forlorn.

Ryan had started 26 games and finished only 3. He relieved in 4. He won only 10 and lost 14. He worked only 152 innings, which were the most he ever worked in New York, but which were not many. He struck out 137, but walked 116, hit 15, and threw 6 wild pitches.

Ryan was wearying of being ridiculed. The telecaster and former player Maury Wills observed, "You can't hit his fastball. Fortunately, you don't have to. He can't get it over." Jim Murray wrote, "They used to say Sandy Koufax could throw a ball through a brick wall. So could Ryan . . . if he could hit it. He would walk the Empire State Building." Ryan remembers, "It began to get to me."

Later he recalled, "Every time I'd get in trouble I'd be taken out. I never relaxed. I never felt I'd be given a chance to get out of trouble. Every time I started I knew if I didn't do well, I wouldn't start again for a while. I was trying too hard and wasn't relaxed. One weekend a month I had to go to my reserve unit, so I was frequently forgotten.

"Sometimes a week would go by that I wouldn't

83

throw a ball. When I got to work, I'd be wild. The Mets developed some fine arms like Tom Seaver's, Jerry Koosman's, and Gary Gentry's, but these are people who didn't have the control problem I had. I usually wasn't wild when I worked regularly. I lost control and went wild when I'd sit out ten days at a time.

"Hodges and Walker should have seen the sort of pitcher I was and gone with me. There just wasn't any communication from Hodges and Walker. I never received any instruction. Seaver tried to help me, but that's not his responsibility. I felt the manager and the pitching coach had no faith in me. I guess they got together with the general manager and decided I wasn't going to do it. I was beginning to wonder myself, but I wasn't ready to give up.

"I felt I was on the verge of a breakthrough. I felt I'd shown them more than enough for them to see it, but I saw they didn't see it in me anymore. I thought all I needed was to work one full season in turn, every fourth day, but I had no idea what they were thinking. They weren't talking to me."

Who knows what they were thinking? Trade talk swirled around Ryan. Rube Walker insisted, "There's no way we'll trade him. Nollie has too much potential. Look at Sandy Koufax and how long it took him to develop. No, they'll never trade this kid."

Ryan said, "I wanted to be traded, but I was hesitant. You never know what's going to be best for your future."

Obviously, if he could have made it with the Mets, he could have made more money in New York than anywhere else. But he had more than money on his mind. He wasn't happy with the way he had been handled by the Mets, and he wasn't happy in New York.

The last month of the 1971 season he suffered, homesick for the happy country life. He remembers, "There was a nice park down the street from our house. When it rained, there wouldn't be anybody in the park, and I'd take Molly, one of my hunting dogs, down there. For some reason, rabbits would come out in the rain, and Molly and I would chase rabbits all afternoon."

He was lost in the big city.

7 California, Here He Comes

On December 9, 1971, Nolan Ryan was at home in Alvin when he was reminded that the next day was the deadline for interleague trading. He remembers, "I thought if I get by tomorrow without being traded, I won't be traded. The Mets could still have traded me within the National League, but I didn't think they wanted to take the chance of my becoming a big pitcher with another National League team and coming in to pitch in Shea Stadium regularly. I figured if I wasn't traded to a team in the American League, I wouldn't be traded. I wanted to be traded, but I worried about where I might go."

The following day he was in a biology class at Alvin Junior College when the class was interrupted and he was told he'd been traded to the California Angels. He, minor-league pitcher Don Rose, catcher Francisco Estrada, and outfielder Leroy Stanton had been traded for veteran infielder Jim Fregosi.

Nolan said, "My first thought was I was one of four players given up for one player. Four for one isn't very flattering, and I was a little embarrassed by that. Then, too, even if you want to be traded, it's usually a little embarrassing if you are. It's as if your team has given up on you, as if you're a failure. And you have to move your wife to a new town and join a new team and meet new teammates. It's unsettling.

"Then, too, I worried a little bit about going to Anaheim. The Mets had become winners, while the Angels were losers. All I knew was Anaheim was near Disneyland and didn't draw many big crowds. The Dodgers did, in their ball park, but not the Angels in theirs. Their stadium was always alive, but I feared Anaheim was dead."

Nolan's concerns were eased somewhat by a call from Harry Dalton, the general manager of the Angels, who told him how happy he and manager Del Rice were to have him on their side and how happy they thought he would be in sunny Southern California. Dalton told him the Angels believed in him. Del Rice called to confirm this. He called 1972 a critical year in Nolan's career in which he could establish himself as a star instead of just one of many mediocre players long regarded as potential stars.

Ryan recalls thinking, "I was either going to establish myself or have another mediocre year. People believed in me. I didn't want to disappoint them. That's why I didn't quit. Deep down inside I knew I threw as well as anyone."

He had not proved it in New York, though he had approached it. After seasons with 6-9, 6-3, 7-11, and 10-14 records he had wound up with a poor 29-38

87

overall record. He had won only 29 of 70 decisions and finished only 13 of 73 starts. He had struck out 493 foes and walked 341 in 510 innings. He had averaged nearly 9 strikeouts every 9 innings, but also had averaged 6 walks and between 3 and 4 earned runs for every 9 frames.

"I've been a disappointment to myself," he said. "I hate to hear people still refer to me as a prospect because after four years in the majors I should have achieved more than I have. I'm not a prospect, but neither should I be a suspect. If I didn't feel I had the potential to be a twenty-game winner, I'd quit."

Fregosi was traded to the Mets only because the Angels' new general manager, Harry Dalton, wanted to make them over into his own team. He had a new manager, Del Rice, who would be the boss on the field. The only remaining original Angel, Fregosi was a smart baseball man who had the potential of managing.

The old cowboy movie star Gene Autry and his partner, former Stanford football star Bob Reynolds, owned the Angels, who had come into existence as an expansion team in 1961. Fred Haney was their first general manager, followed by Dick Walsh, and Bill Rigney was their field manager into their tenth season.

After finishing eighth their first season, they made a surprising bid for a pennant their second season before fading to finish a respectable third. They could not recapture that magic, however, and finished as high as fifth only twice in the next six seasons.

For a while such youngsters as Fregosi, Albie Pearson, Leon "Daddy Wags" Wagner, Lee "Mad Dog" Thomas, Bob Rodgers, Bobby Knoop, Bo Belinsky, and Dean Chance appeared to be potential superstars, but all paled in one way or another. Chance won the Cy Young Award in 1964, but faded.

Rigney was removed and replaced by Lefty Phillips early in the 1969 season, and the team spurted. The Angels finished third that season and an even stronger third the next season, but after falling back to fourth in 1971, Phillips was finished.

Their first year the Angels played in minor-league Wrigley Field. For four years they shared Dodger Stadium.

When Anaheim Stadium had opened in 1967, the Angels had moved into their own beautiful new ball park in suburban Orange County, the fastest-growing county in the country. For four of five years they lured 1,000,000 fans.

Attendance dipped below 1,000,000 in 1971, and Autry instituted sweeping changes. His main move was to hire Harry Dalton away from Baltimore, where he had led the Orioles to three consecutive pennants. Dalton demanded and was given a free hand in deals. The first he engineered was the one for Ryan, surrendering Fregosi, who was Autry's favorite player and influential with him.

Dalton admits, "Mr. Autry could have kept me from unloading Fregosi, but the decision was left to me, and happily we came up with Ryan."

Actually he offered Fregosi around for a pitcher and asked for Gentry from the Mets. The Mets offered Ryan instead. Before the trade could be made, the Mets had to throw in three fringe players, at least one of whom, Stanton, would play a lot for the Angels, though not spectacularly.

Dalton had inherited Rice as his manager, but had

appointed successful college coach Bobby Winkles as Rice's aide and heir apparent. And Winkles, who had tutored Gentry at Arizona State University, gave Gary a big buildup. However, Dalton hints that going after Gentry was strategy designed to trick the Mets into hanging onto him and offering another hurler instead. When the Mets offered Ryan, Dalton grabbed him. "We wanted Nolan all along," Dalton says.

Not everyone in Southern California did. Fregosi was the team's top player. The team already had top starting pitchers in Clyde Wright, Andy Messersmith, and Rudy May. One writer said, "The Angels need another pitcher like Howard Hughes needs a press agent."

Nolan spent the winter worrying about his ability to land a position in the team's starting rotation. Ruth presented him with a son on November 21, less than two weeks after he'd been traded. They named the boy Robert Reid, but called him Reid almost from the first. The three arrived at the Angels' preliminary camp at Holtville in the California desert in February, and Nolan, just turned twenty-five, went to work.

He threw hard from the first. During the first week he said, "Del Rice has encouraged me a great deal, and his pitching coach, Tom Morgan, has talked with me almost as much as Walker and Hodges did all last year."

He sat in the sun and discussed his talent, saying, "I'm wild, but the funny thing is I'm not wild all over. I'm not wild inside or outside. I'm not wild low. I'm generally just wild high. But I never worked more than one-hundred-fifty-two innings in any season in New York. I never got grooved. With the Mets, I felt I had to prove myself every chance I got. Here I've been told I'll pitch regularly and get plenty of chances. I don't feel the pressure I felt in New York.

"I feel I'm getting a fresh start, and that feels good. I want to wipe out the past. I'm looking forward to the future."

After the team pitched its permanent preseason camp in Palm Springs and started along the exhibition trail, Ryan worked regularly whether he was effective or not.

However, privately Ryan remained unsure of his future in baseball at that point in his career. Ruth Ryan recalls, "He was wild that spring and worried that he would never reach his potential as a pitcher. Our baby had been born that winter, and Nolan was worried about me and Reid. We couldn't afford to rent a house in Palm Springs, where the Angels trained, so Nolan was driving two hundred and fifty miles round trip every day to Anaheim, where we'd already rented a house. Some of the players were striking. It was a very discouraging situation, and we felt sorry for ourselves. He came close to quitting and if the strike hadn't ended soon, I'm sure he would have. I remember him saying, 'Why don't we just go home?' But I said we should stick it out so he could give it one more good chance, and he did."

Once the team started along the exhibition trail, Nolan worked regularly, but he was wild, so wild that when he struck a San Francisco batter with a pitch, it ignited a brawl with the Giants. But the Angels kept pitching him whether he was effective or not. Managing the team at the time, Del Rice now admits, "Often he was very wild and inconsistent. I was pessimistic about the trade. But this was the type of fellow you had to stick with because of his great potential. He can throw like Koufax. Koufax took a long time to develop, too. People forget that."

Koufax was in the majors six seasons before he won as many as a dozen games any season. But his first three seasons he didn't start as many as 15 games any season, and his next three he didn't start as many as 30. He was swift, but wild, and the Dodgers didn't depend on him. He was worked irregularly and couldn't control his talent. He considered quitting. His early years were remarkably like Ryan's.

The first season Sandy got 30 starts and 200 innings, he became a winner. So would Nolan.

"It's hard to believe that Sandy went through the same things that I'm going through," Ryan observed. "I only saw him late in his career when he made pitching look easy. I guess the suffering now will make success that much more enjoyable—if it comes."

It was not clear it would come, but Ryan recognized he was running out of opportunities and was determined to make the most of this one.

8 An Angel Ace

Nolan Ryan's first start as an Angel came in the third game of the 1972 season. The California club was at home at Anaheim in chill weather before a small turnout of fewer than 6,000 fans. Ryan outpitched Jim Perry and shut out the Minnesota Twins, 2–0. He walked five and hit one, but struck out 10.

Nolan had not pitched for eighteen days following his wild ways in the late March exhibition game against the Giants but had turned out for a special workout the very next day, had profited from tips offered by catcher Jeff Torborg, and had been working hard daily since. "I feel like I've found something, like I've got a handle on it," he observed happily later in the dressing room.

But it wasn't that easy to pin down, and it got away from him for a while. On the road he went erratic again. He lost in Texas and was blasted in Baltimore. Back home, he blanked Milwaukee but then, after retiring his first 13 foes, strained a groin muscle and was batted out by Boston.

He lost a tough, 2–1 contest to Oakland and Blue Moon Odom, but dazzled the A's. But then he was hammered by the A's in Oakland. It took him forty minutes to get out of the first inning as he walked four and threw a wild pitch.

At 2-4 in mid-May he was in trouble. Manager Rice talked to pitching coach Morgan about assigning Ryan to relief duty. After all, he had the fastball which could be a reliever's best weapon. And he had come out of the bullpen before in that brief but brilliant pair of post-season efforts for the Mets a few years earlier.

Morgan was wise, however. He knew Ryan dreaded relief duty—and was too wild to be effective in relief. He suggested he would work with Ryan between starts and on off days if Rice would go along with him a little longer. The team was losing more games than it was winning and was fast falling from the race, but Rice recognized Ryan's potential and agreed.

Ryan certainly agreed. Morgan enlisted the help of Roseboro and catchers Torborg, John Stephenson, and Art Kuysner, and they worked with the wild young man regularly, at home and on the road, often in otherwise-deserted ball parks.

Nolan struggled to a victory over Kansas City, then shut out Chicago at home. He gave up 7 hits and walked 4, but struck out 10 and was strong in tight spots. He was so fast at times that four former Dodgers who were on hand compared him to Koufax.

Lefty Phillips, Dodger pitching coach when Koufax was at his best, said, "Ryan's faster than Koufax."

Torborg, who caught both, said, flatly, "Ryan is faster. I never expected to catch anyone as fast as Sandy, but Nolan is faster. I got a bone bruise on my hand on his third pitch of the game. The big glove isn't enough protection. The last time that happened to me was when I caught Koufax's perfect game. Ryan will throw no-hitters, too, you watch!"

John Roseboro, who caught Koufax, said, "Ryan can throw anything Koufax could. It's a question if he can do it consistently. If he'll let up a little on his fastball, he'll be more consistent."

Del Rice, who caught some of the best, said, "If he'd take a little off, he'd be the best in baseball."

Tom Morgan said, "He's starting to take a little off. He's going to be the best."

The first week in June, in Detroit, Nolan had a no-hitter after four innings, but Norm Cash got a two-base hit to start the fifth. However, Ryan allowed only three hits and walked only two in winning, 4–1. Morgan said, "He's been faster, but he's seldom been better. He's learning how to pitch." Rice said, "At this rate, he's going to be one of the best ever."

A week later he whipped Cleveland. But then he lost a three-hitter to Detroit and Mickey Lolich, 2–0. At Oakland he stifled the A's on two hits, 2–1. At Minnesota he beat the Twins, 3–1. Some of the Twins were wary of his fast, tight pitches. "If he ever hits me with a fastball, I'll have him arrested for manslaughter," the great Harmon Killebrew said, smiling—but just a little. Roseboro observed, "Ryan scares batters the way Koufax never did because Sandy never threw close to a batter and now Nolan does."

At home against Oakland in his first start in July, Ryan terrified the A's. He equaled his career record and set a club record with 16 strikeouts as he hand-cuffed the league leaders, 5–3. He allowed just five hits and three walks. But he hit two, and a wild pitch brought in one run.

He struck out Dave Duncan four times and Sal Bando three times. Duncan said, "I saw the ball, but I couldn't get my bat on it." Bando said, "He threw me one ball I didn't even see." Reggie Jackson, the super-slugger, said, "He's the only man in baseball I'm afraid of. If one ever gets away from him, he can kill someone."

After a loss to Milwaukee on the Fourth of July, the traditional midway mark in the season, the Angels had won 32 games and lost 40 and had fallen 15 games behind the A's in the Western Division of the American League. Outfielders Vada Pinson and Ken Berry, first baseman Bob Oliver, and second baseman Sandy Alomar were playing well, but no one was producing power. Runs were scarce, and the pitchers were struggling. Clyde Wright was pitching consistently, as was Ryan, but Rudy May was inconsistent, and Andy Messersmith was injured.

The next night, Ryan collected his tenth victory as against five defeats with a four-hit, four-walk 1–0 shutout of visiting Milwaukee.

At that point he assessed his season and said, "This ball club has done the one thing I needed, which was to pitch me in turn regularly. They let me pitch every four days, and as a result, I have learned a lot about pitching. The Mets would have buried me in the bullpen when I went bad, but the Angels stuck with me and kept trying to help me."

He was putting it all together, and he was brilliant the second Sunday in July with Boston in town. He walked the first batter he faced on four pitches. But he struck out the second. He was to strike out 16. He gave up a single to the third batter, Carl Yastrzemski, who could single off anyone. But it was the only hit Ryan would surrender all night. He retired the next 26 batters in a row. At one point he set a new league record by striking out 8 in a row. He became one of the few pitchers in history to strike out the side on nine pitches when he got Carlton Fiske, Bob Burda, and Juan Beniquez in a row in the second inning. It was the second time he had turned this trick. Immortals Lefty Grove and Sandy Koufax were the only others ever to do it twice, but Ryan was the first to do it in each league. Actually Ryan got all his outs on strikeouts through the first three innings.

He threw 13 straight strikes at one point and 86 in the game, while missing on only 38 balls. It was the second one-hitter and third 16-strikeout contest of his career and his best ever for control. The Red Sox have a hard-hitting team, but Ryan had them at his mercy, blanking them, 3–0.

It was his fifth shutout, fifth straight complete game, fifth straight victory, and ninth in his last ten decisions. He had a one-hitter, two two-hitters, two three-hitters, and a four-hitter in that stretch. He had taken over the league strikeout record from Detroit's Mickey Lolich with 138 and stretched his string of consecutive scoreless innings to 21.

When he was finished, his foes were awed. Leadoff batter Tommy Harper said, "He walked me, but I was surprised he didn't knock me down. He's so wild sometimes he scares you, especially at the start of a game before he gets into a groove. The first time up I saw the ball leave his hand, and then I didn't see it again. I

97

heard it—zing! It hit the screen behind home plate about the time I hit the dirt. When he was zipping that ball across the strike zone, we were helpless to hit it."

Yastrzemski said, "I swung, and I happened to hit the ball. I didn't get a good look at it. I didn't get a good piece of another pitch all night. He throws as hard as anyone. On nights like tonight when he isn't wild, there's almost no way you can beat him." Manager Eddie Kasko said, "Sometimes he beats himself. The way he's throwing, if he doesn't, not many will."

Ryan said, "It was the best game I have ever pitched. In my previous one-hitter and sixteen-strikeout games, I was wilder. Tonight I was as fast as I've ever been, but the ball was going where I wanted it to go. When I can put it where I want it, I feel very confident."

New York's loss had turned out to be Anaheim's gain. Ryan, Ruth and Reid had rented a one-story split-level house with a patio and a swimming pool in the Anaheim area. There was a Ping-Pong table and a barbecue unit on the patio. The weather was wonderful. They were outside the smog belt. "It's not Texas, but it's more my way of life than New York could be," said Nolan.

Southern California had taken to him. He was hot, and especially hot at home, where he had won eight out of ten decisions, pitched all five of his shutouts, and given up only one earned run a game.

The team was a disappointment. At the halfway point in its schedule it was to have a 36–45 record and be 14 games out of first place. But Ryan was a stunning attraction. His starts were luring 2,000 to 4,000 fans above the average at home. Away from home he was worth 4,000 to 6,000 extra in attendance. "He's becoming the biggest gate attraction in baseball," Dalton observed.

This put a lot of extra pressure on him, but Nolan was enjoying his first true prominence. "I'm having a good time." He grinned. "I wish the team was going better, but I'm glad I'm going good."

The New York press came in with the Yankees, and Ryan was almost smothered by attention from writers and broadcasters, who had been busy blasting Met management for letting this sensational young man go. Jim Fregosi was not hitting and had been benched, turning the trade into a terrible one. Vida Blue had held out, reported late, and was having a horrible year. Nolan Ryan was the pitching sensation of his sport. "I believe I could be pitching just as well for the Mets if I were still with them," Nolan told the New York press.

His turn did not come against the Yankees, but it did in Milwaukee, where he was beaten, 7–3, to start a road trip on July 14. It was his first loss since June 18. He had given up only six home runs in his previous 125 innings, but he was hit for three in these nine innings, including a two-run homer and a grand slam by Johnny Briggs. Ryan gave up as many runs as he had given up in his six previous games. He pitched his tenth complete game, but a bad game.

The next outing, in Boston, he was batted out in seven innings and beaten 4–1. Red Sox slugger Carl Yastrzemski observed, "He was just missing the plate tonight, and we could wait him out. He was only two or three inches away from what he was the last time we saw him, but in this game that can be a big difference." In New York, he was routed, 7–1. "He's the same old Ryan," the reporters there wrote, to Nolan's deep disappointment.

Selected for the All-Star game, but slumping, he was not used in Atlanta as the National League won, 4–3. "It was a thrill just to be there," he said.

He returned to action at home against Texas and two-hit the Rangers, shutting them out, 5–0, to snap his three-start slump. Ryan fanned 14 in recording his sixth shutout and twelfth triumph. He had a no-hitter until two were out in the eighth inning, when Larry Blittner doubled. Bill Mason singled in the ninth for the only other hit off Ryan, who walked only three.

The crowd was roaring on every pitch most of the way, but if they were disappointed to see another no-hit bid fall short, they seemed satisfied by the show he put on for them. Catcher Torborg said, "He'll get a no-hitter yet. And maybe more than one. On a night when he's right, it's hard to hit him."

In the dressing room Rudy May pointed to him and said, "That's greatness." From then on, some called him Greatness.

In his next start, on the last day of August, at home against Kansas City, Ryan trailed from the fourth inning on, when his errors resulted in a run for the Royals, but did not give up a hit until the eighth inning, when leadoff hitter Steve Bovley singled to center. In the home half Ryan was removed for a pinch hitter and wound up losing, 1–0. "I'm disappointed about losing a no-hitter, but more disappointed about losing a game," a weary Ryan said later.

He lost his next three decisions, 1–0 to the White Sox, 4–3 to Cleveland, and 2–0 to Detroit. He had to pitch a shutout to win, it seems, so he did, in his next start, 2–0, at Baltimore. And the start after that, 2–0 at Detroit. And the start after that, 4–0, at Anaheim against Detroit. With the three straight shutouts he stretched his streak of scoreless innings to 34 as August ended and the season moved into its final full month.

Starting September with 15 victories, he was shooting for a 20-victory season: a magic mark for major-league hurlers. On the fourth day of the final month his shutout string ended, but he stifled the A's in Oakland, 2–1. In Chicago he was foiled, 5–1. Back home against Texas, he was stopped, 3–0. The next out, against Chicago, he was shaded, 2–0, for his fifteenth defeat. It was the sixth time his team had been shut out behind him, and he could be excused if he felt frustrated. "You just have to keep trying," he said with a sigh.

Kansas City came in, and he cut them down, 4–2, for his seventeenth victory. The team took to the road, and in Texas, Ryan three-hit the Rangers, 2–1, for his eighteenth triumph. In the process he struck out 12 to take the major-league strikeout lead from the Phils' Steve Carlton and became the seventh man in American League history to strike out 300 or more men in a single season. He had two starts left to go for his 20 victories.

On the season's last Saturday night Ryan set personal and team records and tied the American League night-game mark as he struck out 17 Minnesota batters at Anaheim to win victory number 19 with a five-hit 3–2 triumph. He had to be tough to get this one. He had allowed only two hits and one walk and seemed sure to get his tenth shutout of the season after eight frames but faltered in the ninth.

With one out, Steve Thompson and Steve Braun singled. Harmon Killebrew was walked to load the bases. But the Angels went with Ryan in such situations, as the Mets had not. Bobby Darwin singled in one run to make it 3–1. Still, the Angels stuck with Ryan. A walk forced in a second run to make it 3–2. Ryan reached back and struck out Rick Renick to end the game.

"It's a good feeling when your team puts trust in you," a relieved Ryan said later. He had become the team's top winner, surpassing steady Clyde Wright, who settled for 18 triumphs.

But on the fourth night of October, the season's final game, Ryan was foiled in his bid for his twentieth win in a frustrating 2–1 defeat to Blue Moon Odom and the newly crowned divisional champion Oakland A's, who were to go on to win the world title.

Lack of control and fundamental failure cost Ryan the contest. He walked Reggie Jackson in the fourth inning. Campy Campaneris was sent in to run for Reggie and promptly stole second and then third and then scored on a single by Gonzalo Marques. In the seventh a walk, a wild pickoff attempt, and a single produced the decisive run. It was a typical Ryan defeat.

He had allowed just five hits and three walks in his sixteenth loss. The team had not scored any runs in six of his losses in which he surrendered only 10 runs. He had lost three other games by one run. He lost two games by 1–0, two by 2–1, and three by 2–0. "He could have won twenty-five to thirty games," Dalton declared later.

The Angels scored the fewest runs in the league in winning only 75 games of the strike-shortened 155-game schedule. He had started 39 games and completed 20 in putting together a 19–16 record that was better than it appeared.

He shut out nine teams, and his earned run average was a superlative 2.28. Opponents were held to a mere .170 batting average against him, lowest in the league. Next lowest was the A's Catfish Hunter, who held opposing players to a .189 mark.

Significantly, he worked 284 innings, almost twice that of any of his prior seasons.

The fireballer did have his troubles. He walked 157 batters, hit 10, and uncorked 18 wild pitches. But he got the 7 strikeouts he needed in his last start to surpass Sam McDowell's 325 as the fourth highest single-season total in major-league history.

The crowd cheered the twenty-five-year-old fireballer as he left the field for the last time in 1972. In the dressing room the weary young man sighed wistfully and said, "I'm disappointed at the defeat. I wanted that twentieth victory. But it's been a good season for me. I'll just have to pitch better."

Incredibly, he did, the very next season.

9 No-Hit Nolan

Baseball is a team game, and one player cannot win titles for his team—not even a superpitcher such as Nolan Ryan became in the early 1970's. But he did become the most important performer by far on the California Angels, if not in all baseball.

Attendance in Anaheim had dipped to 744,000 in 1972, second lowest in the team's twelve years and lowest in seven seasons in its own stadium, but Ryan's brilliance restored interest. Attendance increased more than 250,000 in 1973.

Hitting in the .230's for the second straight season, Jim Fregosi was sent to Texas by the Mets, admitting their mistake. Meanwhile, the Angels had been given a great gift in Nolan Ryan. He had become the cornerstone of the club's efforts to rebuild. In a major trade general manager Harry Dalton dealt pitcher Andy Messersmith and infielder Ken McMullen to his area rivals, the Dodgers, in return for outfielder Frank Robinson, outfielder-infielder Bobby Valentine, infielder Billy

Grabarkewitz, and pitchers Bill Singer and Mike Strahler.

The smart, talented thirty-eight-year-old veteran Robinson set club records with 30 home runs and 97 runs batted in to increase club scoring enormously. His career total of home runs reached 552, outranked only by Babe Ruth, Henry Aaron, and Willie Mays. But the hustling Valentine suffered a severe broken leg crashing into an outfield fence in his thirty-second game and was lost for the season. Grabarkewitz seemingly couldn't buy a hit and was sent away at midseason. Only Bob Oliver, who hit 18 homers and drove home 89 runs, supported Robinson at the plate. Outfielders Vada Pinson and Ken Berry were ordinary.

The handsome, hard-throwing Singer was sensational. A twenty-game winner for the Dodgers in 1969, he had suffered a series of injuries and lost his touch, but he bounced back as an Angel with 20 victories and 241 strikeouts in 1973 to provide splendid support for Ryan, who won 21 games and fanned 383. Their two-man total of 624 strikeouts was tops in history. They were by far the best two-man starting unit in the sport. But there were no winners behind them. May was talented but disappointing, winning 7 and losing 17. The rest couldn't come close.

Rice had been removed, and Dalton brought in Bobby Winkles, who had turned out such future professional standouts as Reggie Jackson and Sal Bando and collegiate team champions at Arizona State. However, his rah-rah tactics turned many of the top pros against him. An old-fashioned gentleman, he seemed out of touch with the times. While the A's were soaring to their second straight world title behind beards, mustaches, and the freedom to fight and argue among themselves, the Angels were finishing fourth, 15 games short, with short hair, clean shaves, and restrictive rules.

Of course, the A's had superplayers in their prime, while the Angels had only a Ryan and a Singer at their peak. Winning 79 games and losing 83, the California club struggled through another disappointing season, brightened mainly by the brilliance of Ryan, who, with Singer and Robinson, kept the team respectable and in the race for more than half the season before the club collapsed during the dog days of July.

The Angels were a bit better than a .500 team for the first half of the season, but Ryan was only a .500 pitcher. He got off to a fast start before he fell back on bad ways, bothered by a bad back which lingered through the season.

Nolan thrilled more than 27,000 fans as he outpitched Jim Busby to beat Kansas City, 3–2, on six hits, striking out a dozen, on opening night. He came back with back-to-back five-hitters to trim Minnesota, 4–1 in Anaheim and 3–2 in Minnesota, striking out 11 in the first one and 14 in the second to give him three straight victories at the start of the season.

He went eight innings in Oakland without getting a decision as the A's won in the tenth, 3–2. Then he was knocked out in the seventh in a 6–2 defeat against Cleveland at Anaheim to absorb his first loss of the new campaign. He struggled twelve innings, surrendering 10 hits, en route to credit for a 5–3 triumph over Detroit in his first start in May. He was wild and threw 205 pitches, which is about 50 more than is acceptable.

One pitch was a fastball when catcher Torborg was

expecting a slow curve. Surprised by the speed of the pitch, Torborg was taken out with a bruised wrist and had to be replaced. "My wrist took the worst of it, but it got all of me," the catcher commented later. "You could use armor receiving that guy."

Ryan remained wild in Baltimore. He gave up only three hits in seven innings, but walked seven batters before he was removed from a 5–0 defeat. "It's an old story with me. I'm out of kilter. I've got to find the groove again," Ryan reported. New manager Winkles said, "With his talent, it's too soon to worry."

But he was worried, and after five of the first six batters Ryan faced reached base and scored on him in a game against Chicago at Anaheim, he was removed from what wound up a 7–4 defeat and sent to the bullpen in search of his touch. He came back the very next night to toss three innings of four-strikeout, two-hit shutout ball in a 6–5 win over the White Sox and was restored to the rotation. Dalton wasn't about to see his best pitcher buried because of a slump.

The slump ended spectacularly in Nolan's next start on Tuesday night, May 15, in Kansas City's fantastic new futuristic park in a game televised as well as broadcast back to Southern California. He was simply overpowering. He pitched a no-hitter. The only near hits for the Royals were a looping pop fly to left-center that almost landed between shortstop Rudy Meoli and center fielder Valentine, which Meoli caught in his outstretched glove on the run with one out in the eighth, and a long fly to right, which Berry bagged easily enough, though only three feet short of the fence, for the last out in the ninth. Otherwise, the Royals did not come close to a hit. Their only runners were walked on board—Steve Hovley in the first, Carl Taylor in the third, and Paul Schaal in the eighth.

Ryan had not won a game or struck out as many as 10 batters in a game in five starts over two weeks. Throwing mostly sizzling fastballs, but also breaking off a sharp curve at times, Nolan struck out 12 Royals, at least one in every inning, as he won this one. His foes seemed frustrated as they started to swing wildly at his fast stuff after a while. In fact, the Royals were so frustrated that manager Jack McKeon later insisted Ryan was coming off the rubber and throwing from a foot in front of it most of the way, but umpire Jim Evans just laughed and said, "It just looked that way." Slugging John Mayberry said, "He threw the ball harder than any man I ever saw in my life." Hal McRae suggested, "If there's a higher league, he should be in it. On nights like this, he's too good for ordinary major leaguers." Shortstop Freddie Patek asked in awe if this was Ryan's first no-hitter. Told it was, he said, "Well, it won't be his last."

He was right, too.

With Bob Oliver homering for one run and singling in another, Ryan rode a 3–0 cushion to the completion of his gem, while more than 12,000 fans turned from rooting for their team to cheering the hurler onward to immortality through the last, tense outs. At the finish Ryan was surrounded by his teammates and escorted with hollering happiness to the dressing room. "I never thought I'd get one, but at the end I was sure going for it," Ryan said, grinning, as the press poured over him.

Catcher Torborg, who had predicted more than one for Ryan, who had caught no-hitters from Koufax and

Singer while with the Dodgers, and who now had received his third gem, seemed especially ecstatic. "Oh, God, that was beautiful," he said. He couldn't stop clapping his hands. "This was as good as any of 'em." Embracing her husband later, Ruth Ryan said, "It was great, just great." Two-year-old Reid Ryan had little to say.

Clyde Wright and Bo Belinsky had pitched previous no-hitters for the Angels. Many hurlers have thrown no-hitters, but Dizzy Dean never did, nor did Grover Cleveland Alexander, Lefty Grove, Rube Waddell, and many other immortals. Sandy Koufax threw four and Bob Feller three, but few throw even two. Only one man ever threw two in a row, Johnny Vander Meer in 1938, the second one in the first night game ever played in the majors.

Inevitably, Vander Meer's incredible performance was recalled when Ryan made his next start four nights later in Anaheim against Texas and pitched another no-hitter for three innings. He lost it when Mike Epstein sliced a double just fair along the left-field foul line to open the fourth. But Nolan allowed only three more hits and fanned a dozen en route to an easy 9–1 win.

With his two innings of hitless relief prior to his no-hitter and his three innings following, Ryan flung 14 hitless frames before being reached for a safety. Afterward he was philosophical. He smiled and said, "It takes a lot of luck to get one no-hitter, much less two in a row. I'll admit I thought about it. Maybe I'll get another shot at it another time."

Not right away, however. He lost his next three starts—4–1 to Chicago, 2–1 to Boston, and 2–0 to

New York. He bounced back to blank Detroit on five hits, 3–0, but then was beaten by Boston, 6–5. He stopped New York, 5–2, but then was crushed by Chicago, 8–3. He five-hit Kansas City, 5–2, but then lost six-hitters, 4–0 to Minnesota and 3–0 to Oakland.

On the Fourth of July the Angels were respectable at 41-37, only two games from first. They had even led for two days a few days earlier. But Ryan was struggling erratically. "I feel I'm riding a roller coaster," he commented wistfully.

He was hit hard and needed relief help in the ninth but got credit for a 3–1 victory in Cleveland, which squared his record at 10-10. Meanwhile, Singer was sizzling and reached a record of 14-4 with an easy victory the next day, which put the Angels at 43-38, still two games from first, at the exact midseason mark in their schedule.

Ryan was slugged out in six innings of a 7–1 loss in Baltimore in his next start. But, typically of his up-and-down performances this season, he bounced back brilliantly in his following effort, his second no-hitter of the season, Sunday afternoon, July 15, two months to the date from his first.

This like the first one was in Detroit. Ryan was spectacular. His fastball was taking off as if it were hitting bumps, and his curveball was breaking as if it were rolling off a tabletop. He had good control, walking only four and throwing only 45 bad balls to 81 strikes. Ryan struck out 16 of his foes in the first seven innings, and had a shot at the all-time record of 19 for a single game. But during a five-run Angel eighth, providing the padding for his 6–0 triumph, his arm stiffened up. He was able to strike out only one more the rest of the way, though that was enough to match his career high of 17 for one contest. The only hard-hit ball off him came with one away in the ninth, when Gates Brown ripped a rising liner which shortstop Rudy Meoli speared a foot above his head.

Norm Cash followed with a pop-up in the infield to Meoli, and the big crowd cheered the enemy ace who had so sensationally subdued their Tigers to become one of the few pitchers ever to hurl two no-hitters in a single season. After the last out his Angel teammates surrounded Nolan ecstatically.

Ryan now had 26 straight scoreless innings against Detroit. As Tiger manager Billy Martin put it, "He's always good against us, but this is the best I've ever seen him. He had everything." The Tiger players praised him as highly as Martin did.

Ryan's 17 strikeouts were the most ever in a no-hitter. With them, he equaled the American League record of 30 strikeouts in two straight games and surpassed one of 41 in three games in a row, both established by Sudden Sam McDowell. But it was the opportunity he now had to match Vander Meer's mark of two straight no-hitters and to become the first man ever to throw three in a single season that had everyone excited. "I think I have a shot at it," Nolan predicted.

He did. It was in Anaheim against Baltimore before shrieking fans. Three innings. Six innings. A seventh. The tension was almost unbearable as the excitement increased batter by batter. He walked some and threw some wild pitches. In fact, a walk, steal, wild pitch, and groundout gave the Orioles a run in the opening inning, but as he headed into the eighth, the game tied, 1–1, he still had not given up a hit.

Ryan hit leadoff batter Brooks Robinson with a pitch to open the eighth. Shortstop Mark Belanger came up. Batting ninth in the order, a weak hitter averaging .215 without a homer all season, Belanger was in an obvious bunting situation. He did indeed try to bunt on the first pitch—and missed. He figured to try for at least one more strike but suddenly stepped back and swung as Nolan fired a fast one. Belanger barely hit the ball and looped a soft fly to short left-center. Ken Berry, playing to the right of center, made a run for it, but it fell at his feet, safely.

It was not much of a hit—but it was a hit. Ryan's shoulders seemed to sag, and he turned away in disappointment, but the crowd came up to give him a standing ovation in appreciation of his enormous effort. Then Ryan returned to work. He struck out Al Bumbry, struck out Rich Coggins, and got Tommy Davis to fly out to center to strand the two runners and preserve his tie. Again the crowd came to its feet to cheer him for his clutch hurling. He had hurled 16 straight hitless innings before Belanger's bloop hit.

In the ninth Nolan fanned Elrod Hendricks and the scoreboard reported he had tied one Sam McDowell record with 31 strikeouts in two straight games and broken another with 41 in three straight nine-inning games. He wrapped up a nine-inning one-hitter, but the game remained tied as the teams went into extra innings. Belanger got another bloop hit in the tenth, a squibbler that settled in short right between the reaches of the second baseman and right fielder, but Ryan retired the side without a score.

The first solid hit off Ryan came in the eleventh

when, with one out, Tommy Davis doubled down the left-field line off the tiring pitcher. Winkles removed Ryan at this point, and Nolan waved wearily to the crowd in appreciation of yet another standing ovation as he walked off. Surely the record for standing ovations in a single game was set in this one. But that was the last hurrah for this night. Dave Sells came in, got one out, but then gave up a walk and a two-run double by Terry Crowley.

Ryan and the Angels, lost, 3–1, in a game which went into the books merely as a three-hitter, but had come close to a second-straight no-hitter.

Belanger admitted later, "It was a lucky hit. I'm sure Ryan was expecting another attempt at a bunt."

Oriole manager Earl Weaver, who had the umpires inspect Ryan's glove for grease or other sticky substance in the seventh inning in an effort to get the pitcher ejected, smiled later and admitted, "I just thought he had to be doing something funny to the ball to make it act the way it was. And if it shook him up, well—that's baseball. But it didn't shake him up. He just kept throwing that fastball, and it just kept doing tricks. He had some kind of stuff."

Ryan said, "I had good stuff, though not like the last game. I don't throw any illegal pitches. I haven't even been accused of it much. The other teams know that. I just throw so hard the ball just naturally moves against the air. The harder you throw, the more the ball may move."

He concluded, "You need at least a little luck to pitch any no-hitters. This time I was unlucky. Because it was a blooper that cost me a no-hitter it hurts a lot. But if I hadn't been trying for a no-hitter I might have won and losing hurts worst of all. When you come right down to it, all that really matters is winning. Without that you're at the bottom of the barrel."

10   On Top to Stay

Following his second no-hitter and the third one that almost was, Nolan Ryan's next outing figured to be in the All-Star game. He almost didn't get to the game. He wasn't picked to the pitching staff by American League manager Dick Williams of the A's, which columnist Melvin Durslag called "an act of arrogance." The upset that was stirred up was calmed when major-league commissioner Bowie Kuhn decided to add a player to each side, thus getting not only Ryan into the game, but also Willie Mays.

Ryan deserved selection originally. He accepted his exclusion without a word of protest, but he was let down and not at his best when he did put in an appearance. He worked two innings and gave up a home run to Pete Rose and a double to Bobby Bonds, but the Nationals already were well on their way to another easy victory in this classic series which they have dominated for years.

Disappointed, Ryan was knocked out in his last two starts in July, taking a loss in one which left him two games under .500 at 11–13 as he swung into the second half of the season. He bounced back to win three of his four starts in August to square his record at 14–14. His only loss was a 2–1 heartbreaker in Baltimore. He fanned 49 in the four games, including 8 straight at one point at Milwaukee to equal his own major-league mark.

Nolan Ryan had struck out 288 batters in 244 innings, and it was becoming clear that he was about to follow Sandy Koufax and Rube Waddell as the third pitcher ever to strike out 300 in consecutive seasons. He had an outside shot at surpassing Sandy Koufax's major-league mark of 382 set in 335 innings in 1965.

This was something of a surprise, since the designated hitter rule had come into the American League in 1973. Nolan said that since he no longer pitched against pitchers, he probably would lose a lot of strikeouts he normally got and could not come close to the record. Koufax fanned pitchers 53 times when he set his record. Ryan fanned pitchers 42 times in 1972.

However, Koufax, reached by telephone at his home near East Holden, Maine, looked at it another way. "Because the pitcher doesn't hit, he doesn't get taken out for a pinch hitter. Because of the designated hitter rule, Nolan now has a chance to go nine innings every start, even when he's losing a close game, and that gives him a good shot at the record. The more innings, the more chance a pitcher has for strikeouts. Every pitcher in the past has had games when he had good stuff but had to go out for a pinch hitter, but that won't happen to Nolan now. I wish him well. I won't be upset if the record is broken. If he can get it, he deserves it."

It was pointed out that by the time Koufax set his record he had conquered his control problems and seldom threw more than 100 to 110 pitches in nine innings. Ryan still was wild and usually threw 130 to 140 pitches a game—and some games many more. Clearly, Koufax was less likely to be worn out at season's end than Ryan. Also, Koufax made 41 starts, while Ryan was not likely to get that many.

Ryan said, "I wouldn't want to risk my arm, but if I'm close to the record entering September, I'll go for it. I go for strikeouts. Some players feel that's part of my problem because by throwing hard most of the time I increase my tendency to be wild. But I don't yet have the control to consistently pitch to spots and let the batter hit balls that can be fielded."

He figured to have about ten starts left. If so, he'd have to win six of them to win 20. He was averaging around 10 strikeouts a start, and he needed a little less than 100 for 383. It was clear if he could keep up his pace, he could top the record, but it would be close.

Perhaps he was pressing, for Nolan was beaten in his next two starts, which seemed to put 20 victories out of reach. He lost at home to Milwaukee, 6–2, and to Boston, 4–0. He was lifted after fanning eight Brewers in six innings and eight Red Sox into nine. When he struck out Carleton Fisk in the second inning of the Boston game, it was Nolan's fourth of the game and three hundredth of the season. He was accorded one of those standing ovations from a turnout of almost 14,000 fans.

Asked about the strikeout record, Ryan said, "It's hard to get excited about it when you keep going out and losing. After losing sixteen games, I'd just as soon not lose another one. If I'm going to win twenty, I may not be able to afford losing another one."

He could not know that then, but he would not lose another one.

Driven by determination, he had one of those great nights in his next start, his last start in August, as he blanked the New York Yankees, 5–0, before frenzied fans at Anaheim Stadium.

Third man up in the first inning, Thurman Munson, popped a short, soft fly to the grass between second base and shortstop. Infielders Sandy Alomar and Ruby Meoli drifted back. Either could have caught it. Both called for it. Each heard the other and pulled up short.

No one went for it. The ball dropped in safely as Munson reached first. He had to be credited with a hit.

It was the only hit the Yankees got. As Ryan went on to hold the Yankees hitless the rest of the way for his fifteenth victory, the simple play seemed a monster.

Munson admitted later, "If it could have been called an error, I wouldn't have complained." Meoli said, "It was a mental error, at least." Alomar admitted, "I feel terrible." Sweat streaming down his flushed face, Ryan said, "It was a bad break. I've had them before. I'll have them again. Anyway, I won."

He won the next one, too, to two standing ovations from fans at Anaheim as he throttled the world champion A's on three hits, 3–1. He struck out 12 to move within 23 of Rube Waddell's American League record of 349 and of Sandy Koufax's National League and major league marks of 382 for single seasons. When he whiffed Campy Campaneris in the fourth inning to finish off Waddell's American League standard of 650 for two seasons, he received his first fan salute. When it was announced at game end that he had reached the fifth highest single-season total ever with 326, he received his second salute. He had another no-hitter until Reggie Jackson singled with two out in the sixth.

This win squared Ryan's record at 16-16 with six starts left. However, Ryan was frustrated in his next start when he fanned four in four innings, but rain washed out the scoreless tie in the fifth inning. The contest was against Kansas City, and all the records of the game had to be removed from the books.

"That probably takes me out of contention for the record," a glum Ryan commented later. "I had four strikeouts. I might have had a lot more. All I can do is keep trying."

The next time, at home against Chicago, he won, 3–1, with 12 strikeouts. He wiped out the White Sox on only four hits, and he was back on the right track.

Four nights later, on September 15, four-month anniversary of his first no-hitter and two-month anniversary of his second no-hitter, the Angels staged "Nolan Ryan Night" and feted him and his wife with gifts. Then he went out and three-hit Kansas City, 3–1, striking out 10, winning his fourth straight game and eighteenth of the season.

On the road in Texas, he five-hit the Rangers, 6–2, but struck out only 7. This set an American League strikeout record for one season but left him 27 short of the major league mark with only two more starts left to him in the rotation.

Both his last two starts were scheduled against the Twins, the first in Minnesota, the second in Anaheim.

In Minnesota Nolan limited the Twins to one hit for

five innings before weariness started to take its toll and he started to stagger. Fortunately for him, the Angels were scoring big that night, and Winkles went with him all the way. The Angels led, 11–0, before Ryan began to weaken, giving up two runs in the sixth and five in the ninth. He surrendered 11 hits in the last four innings and 12 in the game but staggered through to his twentieth victory, 15–7, striking out 12. This gave him twenty-two games in which he had struck out 10 or more opponents this season, which gave him the major-league record, surpassing Koufax's single-season standard.

Now he needed 16 to surpass Sandy's strikeout record for one season. "It was tough, but winning my twentieth was a tremendous thrill," he said later. "I don't know about the strikeout record. If I get ten or eleven at home on Thursday night, I can go for the rest on Sunday afternoon, but I'm about out of steam, and I don't know if I can do it."

He got it, in one of the most exciting games ever seen in Southern California. Reached for three runs in the first inning, he dug deep for stamina and courage and, despite a sore leg, began to blaze the ball past the Twins' sluggers. In the first five innings he fanned 12. In the seventh he got two more. In the eighth, another, Steve Brye, for his fifteenth of the night to tie the great record. By then Ryan was worn out and aching painfully. The crowd, roaring on his every pitch, was limp from the strain of rooting him home.

Nolan surrendered his eighth hit in the ninth but set the side down, though the record strikeout eluded him. Only the fact that the game was tied, 4–4, by that time gave him extra opportunities at the record. The crowd rooted against the batters on both sides, against even the home side, not wanting the game to end before his record quest could end. He gave up his ninth hit in the tenth, but got the side out, though again the record strikeout eluded him.

By then it was a surprise when he was permitted to pitch on. When he went out for the eleventh, the crowd roared with relief, but it was to be his last inning. Of the night and of the season. By then it was unlikely his health would be risked by bringing him back without proper rest on the weekend. He got the first batter on a ground ball, walked the second, his sixth walk of the game, and got the third on a fly. Ten straight batters had survived against him without a "K" recorded in the books.

He had one last chance and made the most of it. The fast one. Reese swung and missed to the crowd's roar. Another fast one. Another swing and another miss and another roar. Base runner Rod Carew broke for second. Catcher Torborg threw. The umpire signaled "safe," and the crowd screamed. Ryan's last chance had not been taken away from him. He threw the fast one again. Reese swung again. And missed. And the arena erupted in cheers as Ryan relaxed in grateful satisfaction. With his last pitch, his 205th of the game, on his last out, he had strikeout 383 of 1973 and a new record for one season.

The Angels won it in the home half for his seventh straight complete-game triumph through the stretch and his twenty-first victory of the season. He lost 16, but for the second straight season his team was shut out in six of his defeats. He lost two games by 2–1 and one by 2–0. Once again he could, with a little luck, have had 25 wins. And with a little luck he could have had four no-hitters. As it turned out, he followed Johnny Vander Meer, Allie Reynolds, Virgil Trucks, and Jim Maloney as the fifth man ever to toss two in one season. And he had two one-hitters and now had four for his career.

In 1973 Nolan started 39 games, completed 26, and worked 326 innings. He set a new record by averaging 10.5 strikeouts every nine innings. He set another new record by totaling 712 strikeouts over two seasons. For his career he now had totaled 1,205 strikeouts, but he really was just beginning. He set or tied seventeen team, league, or major-league records during his most outstanding season so far.

He had four shutouts and a fine earned run average of 2.87. That was only fourth best in the league, however. He was first in the leagues in walks for the second straight season with 162. And with 15 wild pitches and 7 hit batsmen. His career record remained lowly at 69-70. However, he had established himself as a super-pitcher and a consistent winner, who often was more spectacular than any performer in his sport. And he was only approaching his peak.

"I hope to do better in the future," he said.

11 The Country Boy

Following his first no-hitter in 1973, Nolan Ryan was surrounded by reporters. Broadcasters hustled him off first for postgame interviews to the fans in Southern California. Ryan said all the right things. He said he was happy, he said he'd been a little lucky, and he thanked all his teammates for the help they'd given him.

He never criticizes his teammates, even when they make plays behind him that cost him games or even no-hitters. "I make as many mistakes as anyone," he points out. "If the time ever comes when I never throw a wild pitch or walk a batter or throw a fat pitch or make a bad play in the field, I might be entitled to criticize someone else, but I think I'll still understand all players do their best."

Former manager Del Rice says, "He loses his temper sometimes. I remember seeing him throw his glove and kick at the water cooler when I took him out of a game one time, and I was mad because I thought he was mad at me, but then I found out he was just mad at himself for not pitching better. The sort of talent he has—undisciplined and wild, making him inconsistent—is extremely frustrating, but Nolan handles the frustrations well."

Bobby Winkles adds, "It's very hard mentally to pitch a no-hitter or a one-hitter one game and get knocked out of the box in the first inning of the next game, but that's the sort of thing that happens to Nolan, and he handles it real good. Some people think because he's straight and not outwardly emotional, he's not as competitive as he might be, but he's extremely intense inside and demanding of himself. He just holds things in."

Ryan is straight and religious. On the road when he can't get to his regular church at home, he and other ballplayers get together for a religious meeting and "testify to Christ." The Sunday of his second no-hitter the main speaker at the meeting in Detroit was Raymond Berry, former end for the Baltimore Colts. "He didn't talk about winning or anything like that, just about how he found Christ," Ryan reported. "I don't belong to the group, but I go to the meetings on the road. We have on our club a unit of the Fellowship of Christian Athletes, and we hold meetings every Sunday when we're on the road."

He wears his hair trimmed short and doesn't wear the wild duds favored by some mod players. He says, "I'm against long hair that's unkempt, stringy, dirty. But people who have long hair and take care of it look quite presentable. I've never worn my hair real long. I don't have the type that looks good long."

He is aware of his responsibilities to prominence.

The day after the no-hitter the telephone at his home kept ringing, but Ryan resisted the temptation to take it off the hook. Asked how he felt, he smiled and said, "I feel like a telephone operator." He made appointments with a number of writers and broadcasters for interviews. He said, "It's not that often that I get this much attention that I should let it bother me."

When he arrived with the Angels at International Airport in Los Angeles following his second no-hitter, it was very late, but a gathering of about twenty patient fans were still waiting to see him. A high fence prevented the fans from getting near the team bus, which the players boarded. However, it didn't prevent Ryan from walking fifty yards out of his way to talk to the people and sign autographs until he had to leave.

After his awesome accomplishment, the attention increased enormously. A lot of people have pitched one no-hitter, but not many have pitched two. He had pitched himself into an exclusive class. Calls from all over the country. The demands on his time became tremendous. It is the sort of thing that makes life extremely difficult for superstars. It is easy to say they are well paid for it, but sometimes it seems they never have a moment to themselves.

One writer observed that a no-hit pitcher is supposed to act like a kid surprised by a super present on Christmas morning, but Nolan acted like a lad who'd already peeked into the package. Even his teammates were struck by how coolly he handled the mob scene later. "We couldn't believe how steady you were," Clyde Wright told him.

"I never show much emotion," Ryan admitted. "I'm not sure whether that's good or bad. Sometimes it gives

125

people the idea I'm lackadaisical. I'm not. I'm just not excitable. I try to take things in stride. If you don't get too high in good times, you won't get too low in bad times. My wife is more competitive than I am. I hate to beat her at tennis because she gets so mad."

His wife admits, "I'm much more excitable than he is. I cried when he lost that no-hitter on a pop fly. Once a game is over, he forgets it, but with me it kind of lingers on.

"I try to keep things at home as normal as possible for Nolan, but since he became an important player our life has been hectic. After the second no-hitter, I was getting up with the baby and I opened the door to a television camera crew standing in our driveway. They didn't call, just came over and got Nolan out of bed. But he didn't mind. He takes life as it comes. The pressure doesn't bother him."

Most athletes reach a point where they resent the reporters' demands on their time. Even at times when his telephone rang incessantly with requests for interviews, Ryan was agreeable. "I don't mind talking to reporters, even on days I'm going to pitch. Maybe it keeps me from thinking too much about the game." Nolan laughs. "The only problem is I run out of things to say. I'm colorful on the field, but not off the field.

"It can become a problem, I suppose. I hate to sacrifice my privacy. I'm naturally a very private person. I don't like going out in public. I pitch before big crowds, but I'm not a performer by nature. I prefer family life. I like a quiet life. I like small towns. I prefer the country. I'm not recognized everywhere I go in the Los Angeles area, and I'm just as happy about that."

However, the time had come when he was being

recognized frequently on the streets. And of course, at the ball park he was a celebrity. Crowds surrounded him, and kids demanded autographs from him. Sometimes it seems a player signs enough autographs in a single season to take care of every man, woman, and child in the country.

No matter how much rush he was in, Nolan always took time to sign autographs. "I didn't do it as a kid, myself, but I know kids work hard waiting for players and going after autographs, and I have to assume it means a lot to them, so I take the time to sign for them. As long as they're polite, I don't mind. I'm not a hurried guy, normally. I just do it because I think I should."

His dressing room cubicle normally is overflowing with fan mail. "I average one-hundred-fifty to two-hundred letters a week, two or three thousand a season," he says. "I take 'em home and go through 'em all and pick out anything they want to have autographed personally, like a baseball card or a baseball.

"I used to do it all myself, but now there's too many of 'em. My wife helps, and there's a neighbor lady and several others involved in getting it done. We address all the envelopes and I have a three-by-five picture the ball club furnishes for us to send back to people. If they're fan enough to write me, I guess I can be man enough to answer them," he says.

Even many of his teammates, who have elected him their player representative, can be considered fans. They admit being in awe of him, and some who never will be stars and will not linger long in the majors say they imagine they will be proud forever to be able to say they played with him and were friends of his.

He is so polite, so soft-spoken, so considerate of others' feelings it awes even the experienced writers who cover sports and are accustomed to the difficulties of dealing with some spoiled stars.

For example, Joe Durso of the New York *Times,* who knew Nolan and his wife during their Met days, wanted to say hello to Ruth during a visit to Anaheim with the Yankees. Learning she had been late arriving at the ball park that night, Nolan had someone call the press box during the game to tell the writer where Ruth was sitting so he could go down to visit her.

When Nolan knew that another sports writer was celebrating a birthday he sent him a twenty dollar bill to purchase a present for himself. His generosity is well known. After his third no hitter in the 1974 season, management gave him a $2,000 raise. Ryan responded by writing out a number of $100 checks and slipping them into the lockers of teammates who had played key roles in his big game.

Nolan and Ruth Ryan are an attractive couple who are very close. After his near no-hitter which followed his two no-hitters, she admitted she was leading a suspenseful life in their suburban home. She said she didn't bite her fingernails or take tranquilizers but watched in wonder. The first two she watched on television.

"The first one was really thrilling, but the second one was probably the most exciting thing I've ever seen him do," she said.

Their son, Reid, is growing up fast and strong, a chubby charmer with his parents' good looks. Nolan is a devoted father who loves to play with his boy. Nolan's own father died in 1971, and Nolan deeply regrets his father did not live to see him hit the height of his career.

His mother, Mrs. Martha Lee Ryan, recalls how her husband would get into the family car when his son was pitching and drive around Alvin, trying to pick up the game on his car radio. Sometimes you can pick up distant signals better on car radios, and Nolan Ryan, Sr., often tried and succeeded. "He always would do that. He loved listening to the games," Mrs Ryan recalls.

She took his second no-hitter in stride. "It's nice," she said, "but what I'm waiting for is for him to pitch a perfect game."

She added, "I have six children, and I've lived through so many things with these kids I don't get excited about the things they do any more."

Nolan may be the only contemporary ball player who has used snake oil for a lame back and sore elbows.

"There's an old man back home in Alvin who sent me a bottle of snake oil," he explains. "My wife was having back pains after having the baby. She tried it, and it worked. I don't know whether it was psychological or not, but I tried it, and it worked for me, when I pulled my groin muscle. I gave some to Clyde Wright when he had a shoulder problem, and he said it worked for him."

"I can't explain it, but it did work," says Wright. "I got to calling Nolan Dr. Snake Oil. But I didn't use too much of it because it's hard to get."

"It is hard to come by," Ryan admitted. He has hunted it out himself. Someone said there were a lot of things he'd do for a third strike, but turning over rocks in Texas and listening for rattlesnakes weren't among them.

After hunting rattlers at home, Ryan confessed, "There were only two I didn't see. One was twelve feet away. If he didn't rattle, I wouldn't have seen him till too late." He laughed, "If I have a bad game I can always say I was snake-bit."

The Angels do not encourage Ryan's snake hunting. Nor does he encourage publicity about it. He admits he hasn't asked any doctors why the stuff seems to work. "No, I'd hate to hear what a doctor would say. Probably tell me I was out of my tree."

When a writer called Ryan after Jim Palmer was announced as winner of the Cy Young Award in the American League following the 1973 season, Ruth answered. She said, "He's out working in the back pasture with the dogs. He'll call you when he gets home at dark." Callers frequently find Nolan out in the fields or walking the woods. He is not the sort to wait by the telephone or radio to hear if he has won an award. He is the sort who will call back.

Told Palmer had won with fourteen first-place votes and 88 points to nine first-place votes and 62 points for Nolan, the pitcher admitted, "I'm disappointed, but down deep I thought he'd won. We had similar records. Mine was more spectacular, but he has been more consistent. He was with a winner and I was with a loser. I won't worry about it."

Ryan, his wife, and son live quietly during the off-season. They live at the edge of Alvin on an eight-acre tract down a treelined country lane. They have a small house but are replacing it with a two-story Colonial home. He and his older brother, Air Force Major Robert Ryan, also own a 200-acre ranch near Gonzales, 150 miles away. The Ryans spend weekends there.

Ryan owns two horses, two bulls, and fifty head of cattle. He says, "I've had calves for fifteen years. As a boy I bought them at auction, fattened 'em up, and resold them for spending money. You haven't lived until you've fed a two-day-old calf out of a bottle. When you raise a calf like a puppy, you hate to sell him, but as a kid I really needed the fifty dollars."

In the season the Ryans rent a house in the same Anaheim neighborhood every year because they like to return to the same neighbors. In the off-season, Nolan returns to Alvin, to other members of his family, and to neighbors who are old friends.

"I hunt a lot in the winter and work with my dogs," he says. "We usually get up about six or seven in the morning. I'll take Molly out to one of the ponds and let her work with a canvas training dummy. She's a retriever. Betsy is a pointer, and I work with her on pointing. I hunt quail a lot, but I'd just as soon watch the dogs as shoot. I'm not that big a slayer of game."

He was honored with the Owners' Trophy, selected by his fellow players as the outstanding Angel. And he won the first Joe Cronin Trophy, given in honor of the retiring American League president to the player who produces the top performances on the circuit during a season and reflects credit on his sport. He went to Boston for this one but passed up many invitations for public appearances around the country since he just didn't want to stray from Texas.

He also received a big boost in his seasonal salary from \$44,000 to \$100,000, putting him in select company. Actually, when he was asked after his second no-hitter if he was looking for a bonus or expecting to renegotiate his contract, he said, "No, I don't think I deserve it. I'm supposed to pitch well. When I pitch badly, I don't give them any of my salary back." He did feel he had earned his way to the \$100,000 class after the season but merely noted, "I'm sure they'll be fair. I don't expect any argument."

Dalton noted, "He's not the kind of kid who says, 'I deserve this, and this is what I demand.' "

Ryan said, "I think ballplayers are greedy in some respects. I think a lot of them don't give enough of themselves and expect too much in return. At times I feel the fans don't get their money's worth. Ballplayers should put out. I appreciate what I'm paid, and I want to earn it. I know it won't last forever.

He was still taking college courses, studying taxation and ranching subjects and laying a base on which he might later build a major in veterinary medicine.

"One thing I learned in the minors is that most guys are just hanging around down there to make the money 'cause they don't have anything better to do. It's a sad way to live, and I don't want ball to get that kind of hold on me.

"The security for a pitcher is bad anyway. I've been lucky that I've never had any serious arm problems. My arm seems strong. But you never know. Once your arm goes, they got no further use for you. Even if it doesn't, you're lucky if you last much beyond—say, thirty-two, and I don't plan to stay on as a coach or manager.

"So I decided to go to college, learn how to do something else with the rest of my life. You don't feel you're developing much playing ball, except financially. Along about June or July it's like the Army; you're counting the days until it's over."

This has been especially true because the Angels have been a bad team. And 1974 turned out to be about as bad as it can get.

The California club made some moves which did not work out well. Veteran pitchers Clyde Wright and Rudy May were traded. When Bill Singer required a back operation and was lost for most of the season, the burden of backing up Ryan fell to such promising young men as Frank Tanana, Andy Hassler, and Dick Lange, but they were not ready to bear the burden.

The pitchers seemed to miss the expert receiving of Jeff Torborg, who, along with Vada Pinson, Mike Epstein, Sandy Alomar, and several others, were released or traded. Ellie Rodriguez took over as the regular catcher, and Denny Doyle and Dave Chalk moved into the regular infield and they played well, but it did not pay off.

A series of injuries to key players and Bobby Valentine's failure to recover properly from injury hurt horribly. Bob Oliver was platooned and failed to deliver runs regularly. Frank Robinson, restricted to duty as the designated hitter, provided most of the team's punch, but he could not hit with his past power. He led a veteran clique which allied itself against the restrictive, rah-rah managing of Bobby Winkles.

The team got off to a fast start, then faded fast. Through most of the first half of the season Robinson was not even talking to Winkles. Robinson wanted to

133

be the manager, the first black manager of baseball, and many of the players respected the veteran pro more than they did the recruit from college ranks. (After the season ended, Robinson *did* become the first black manager in major-league baseball—of the Cleveland Indians.)

Rumors that Winkles would be fired ran rampant for more than a month before the ax finally fell at the end of June. However, it was not Robinson who replaced Winkles but Dick Williams, who had led the A's to two straight world titles before he became weary of contending with the A's high-handed owner, Charlie Finley.

Williams took over on July 1, appointed Robinson team captain, and the club promptly lost 10 games in a row. Williams was a good manager. His permissive attitude toward long hair and freedom of spirit were sure to be appreciated by his players. But there were not enough good players. The team had the worst record in baseball when he took it over, and it was bound to be worse before he could pull the team together. The team had come apart and had grown dispirited. Rebuilding was required, which would take time, during which time Dalton's job as general manager would be in jeopardy.

Being surrounded by dissension, lack of confidence, loss of desire, and losing seemed to take their toll of Nolan Ryan. He struggled through a lot of the season, wasting much of his talent. He stood on the dugout steps one evening, watching the thin turnout move into the cement saucer, and observed, "I guess a change had to be made, but in all the feuding and fussing it's been

134

hard to get going. I feel guilty, too. I haven't contributed what I should."

At the start, he was wild, wilder than usual. The twenty-seven-year-old "veteran" won a five-hitter, 5–2, in the opener in Chicago, but walked 10 batters to tie a team mark for one game. He also pitched the home opener in Anaheim, but he gave up three hits, five walks, and seven runs before he was removed without getting an out in the second inning of a 10–2 trouncing. Unveiling for the first time an effective change-up, he was one out away from winning a $100 bet from Winkles by pitching a complete game without walking a man when two of his outfielders ran into each other running after a fly ball in the ninth. Four unearned runs eventually resulted, and Boston beat him.

In Boston he beaned Doug Griffin with a fastball which struck the batter just below the left ear as he bent down and leaned over the plate to bunt. He was taken to the clubhouse before he regained consciousness, then rushed to the hospital. Disturbed, Ryan later admitted, "Anything like that is unsettling. But this is the first time I've knocked anybody out. I don't try to pitch people up around the head. You don't go around jeopardizing lives and careers. He just squared around to bunt and froze."

As it turned out, Griffin was out of action more than a month before he could return to the Red Sox, recovered from the impact of the fastball so feared by batters around the league.

Maybe it made the Boston team gun-shy that night, for 15 of them struck out. Ryan gave up only six hits, but walked seven and hit not just one, but two batters, but still struggled through 167 pitches to a 16–6 triumph. The next time out, Nolan was shelled for seven runs and eight hits in six innings by Baltimore. He walked eight but struck out 10 and allowed only four hits in clipping Kansas City, 2–1. He walked eight, but struck out 12 and allowed only six hits as he overcame Minnesota, 4–2.

A threat to Bob Feller's single-season league record of 204 walks, as well as to his own strikeouts standard, Ryan sought out videotapes of previous pitching efforts in an effort to spot something he was doing different in his delivery but found they'd been erased. United Press International photographer Ernie Schwonk observed, "I don't know anything about baseball, but I can't get the same picture of you I could last year. You're doing something different with your arm." He suggested a study of stills.

Ryan went to the files of Angel publicity director Ed Munson, pulled out his package of photos, and examined them intently. Finally, he felt he had found something. "I found out I was short-arming the ball," he reported. "I haven't been extending my pitching arm properly, coming completely overhand." Seeking to regain his rhythm, he fiddled with his form, and for a while he flashed his former brilliance. He had 10 victories by midseason.

At his best he was, of course, spectacular. On the second day of June he was only two innings away from becoming only the second pitcher in the history of the American League—following Bob Feller—to hurl a third no-hit game. Against Detroit at Anaheim, he held the Tigers hitless for seven innings with the crowd of 16,481 cheering louder with every out—until Ed Brinkman reached first on shortstop Dave Chalk's wild throw to open the eighth, was wild-pitched to second, and scored when Mickey Stanley hit a line-drive single to left with none out, spoiling the shutout as well as the no-hitter.

It was the second time in two seasons Nolan had a no-hitter broken up in the eighth inning. He also gave up a single to Al Kaline in the ninth to settle for a two-hitter. He walked eight, hit one, threw a wild pitch, threw 150 pitches, struck out 11, and won, 4–1.

Reminded that Ryan had been 4-0 against the Tigers the previous season, including a no-hitter, Detroit slugger Willie Horton shrugged and said, "The way he pitched, if he pitched against us all the time he'd be forty to nothing." Ryan said, "It's not them; it's me. If I'm right, I can do well against anyone. I wasn't quite right tonight. I was wilder even than usual. But I had good stuff, and I got stronger as the game went on. I was shooting for the no-hitter. I haven't had one at home yet."

Most pitchers haven't had one anywhere.

The Blazer blistered Boston in Anaheim in mid-June. He was wild at first. He walked six, four in one inning, and had to throw 84 pitches through the first four innings. But he gained control as the game went on. And on and on. He walked only four more. He struck out 16 of the Red Sox in nine innings, before the game went into extra innings. He struck out 19 in fourteen innings to set a personal high but fell short of the league record of 21 for an extra-inning game.

He also fell short of his personal record for pitches in a game. When Winkles talked about taking him out of the game in the dugout after twelve innings, Ryan protested, "But I haven't broken my record yet."

"Record, what record?" Winkles asked.

"Most pitches in a game," Ryan said with a grin.

Winkles let him pitch one more inning before mercifully removing him to protect his arm. Ryan, who had thrown 235 pitches, missed out on his mark by 6. He almost certainly would have got it, and the victory as well, had he been allowed to go two more innings, in which the Angels won the marathon, 4–3, with reliever Barry Raziano getting credit for the triumph. Luis Tiant, a clever pitcher who threw a lot fewer pitches, went all the way, a luckless loser when Denny Doyle doubled home the winner in the last of the fifteenth.

It was Ryan's forty-fifth 10-strikeout game in Anaheim and sixtieth in his career. Ryan tied a record by striking out leadoff hitter Cecil Cooper six times in the contest. "I guess you could say he's got my number. Or rather numbers," said Cooper. "It's strikes one, two, and three."

After Whitey Herzog took over as interim manager before Dick Williams could arrive to replace the fired Bobby Winkles, Ryan restored order to a scrambled situation with one of his extraordinary efforts.

Alex Johnson of Texas lined a single to right with two out in the first inning. And it was the only hit Nolan allowed the entire game. Ryan has thrown harder, but never with a better curve or better control. For the first time in his recorded history, he got by on less than 100 pitches—99, to be exact. He came close to that perfect game his mother wanted. He walked only one, was supported errorlessly in the field and faced only 29 in winning, 5–0.

A bit better fielding might have saved his no-hitter. The only hit could have been caught. Joe Lahoud, subbing for injured Lee Stanton, ran in for it, but it fell two feet in front of him. The faster, surer Stanton might have been able to get it. But it was no error, and Ryan had no complaints later.

Except about his bad early-inning luck. It was his fourth one-hitter, and in each of them the one hit had come in the first inning. Johnson joined a select group which also included Denny Doyle, now a teammate of Nolan's, but then a Phil in the National League; Carl Yastrzemski of Boston; and Thurman Munson of the Yankees, who had spoiled gems for Nolan with first-inning hits.

Usually, you have to get to Ryan early if you are going to beat him. In Williams' first game as skipper, Ryan tried his best to give his new manager a victory. He has been sharper, but he was struggling to protect a 3–2 lead against the A's at Anaheim in the eighth, when Sal Bando's double and Nolan's wildness contributed to a two-run rally that put the visitors in front, 4–3. They added another run in the ninth and won, 5–3. However, what this one did more than anything else was point up Ryan's courage in the clutch. A search of the record books revealed that this was the first time in his three seasons and forty-two decisions as an Angel that he had entered the eighth inning ahead and lost.

The next out, he was only seven outs away from that elusive third no-hitter when Cleveland outfielder George Hendrick drove a two-run homer into the left-field bull-pen at the Big A with two out and one on—via an error—in the seventh. That broke a scoreless tie and Ryan's spell. He was knocked out in the ninth of a 7–2

139

loss. Then he was belted out by Baltimore in a 9–1 loss. That was Nolan's low point of 1974. A tough young man, he battled back from there.

He won, 4–2, in Cleveland. He blanked the Orioles in Baltimore, 2–0. He lost a 2–1 heartbreaker at home against Kansas City. He was hit hard but won a decision in a 12–9 game with Minnesota. He lost a 3–2 nod to Chicago. He won in Kansas City, 4–3. He lost a three-hitter in Chicago, 2–1. In this one, an infield hit broke up his no-hitter in the sixth inning.

At home against Boston on August 12, his "heater" was really humming. He fanned five in the first two innings, struck out seven in the middle four frames, then closed with a rush to fan seven more in the final three innings. Winning, 4–2, he became the first pitcher ever to fan 19 batters in two different games.

Ryan had tied the nine-inning major-league mark held by Steve Carlton and Tom Seaver. He had struck out Norm Miller and Bernie Carbo to open the ninth but, after getting two straight strikes on Rick Burleson, had lost on a soft fly ball the twentieth "K" that would have left him all alone in the record books. "I wanted it. I'm satisfied with what I got," Ryan remarked later.

He was not given anything in the game. Only 3 of his 19 strikeouts were "called." Veteran umpire Marty Springsted made Nolan earn every one he got. Later the umpire sighed and said, "They were fouling off his fastballs right at me. I got hit on both sides of my neck and four times in my mask. It hurts. It shakes you up. But I'm not dead yet. I'm a little lucky. Nobody I've ever seen throws as hard."

Ryan topped Milwaukee in his next start. Then, only eight days after his second 19-strikeout game, Nolan threw his third, on July 20 in Anaheim against Detroit. This one went eleven innings, however. And, ironically, Ryan lost it in the eleventh, 1–0, to Mickey Lolich.

Ryan lost another that was tough to take, 2–1, in New York in his next outing, lowering his record to 16–14. He won in Milwaukee, 9–2, in his last start in August. He lost at Oakland, 7–0. Reggie Jackson observed. "He should never be knocked out. He throws so hard he loses control at times. He could throw half as hard and still throw harder than anyone else, and never lose. I haven't seen everyone, but I just know no one ever threw as hard."

Ryan said, "I only know one way to pitch. I am still learning how to pitch, but I think I'll have to throw hard as long as I throw. I don't think I can change. I can't become cute. I don't have that sort of stuff. I have an arm. I have to use it."

How hard did be throw? Seeking to find out, Angel publicists had got in touch with Rockwell International scientists and determined a pitcher's speed could be measured with beams of infrared light. They kept secret a test run on August 20, when one of Ryan's pitches was clocked at 100.9 miles per hour, and bally-hooed a September 7 hosting of Chicago, asking fans to guess his speed. Thousands of guesses from all across the country were received.

Ryan guessed he got faster as games went along. He was right. He threw one pitch at close to 90 mph in the first inning and one or more above it every inning after that. He threw 28 pitches that were measured at above 90 and three that surpassed 100. He threw 8 pitches above 90 in the last inning, and his third pitch of this ninth frame was the topper, clocked officially at 100.8

mph, topping Bob Feller's listed record of 98.6 established in 1946.

Along the way, he cut down the White Sox, 3–1. "I've thrown harder," he said later. "The big buildup got to me. I was a little tense and couldn't concentrate. I was worried I'd try so hard to throw hard I'd blow the ball game."

He wasn't blowing many ball games now. When Williams took over, he tried to establish a five-day rotation for his pitchers. Ryan complained he had to work in normal four-day rotation or lose his rhythm. Now Williams had restored normality, and Ryan was in rhythm.

Nolan four-hit Kansas City, 3–2. He three-hit the White Sox in Chicago, 6–2 for his twentieth triumph of the season. He lost a three-hitter in Minnesota, 3–2. He came back to breeze in Kansas City, 9–3.

With the season coming to a close, Nolan made his last start of September on the twenty-eighth at home against Minnesota. It was a Saturday night. And he was sensational. He was wild, walking eight. But he was overpowering. He didn't give up a hard-hit ball all night. He didn't give up anything that came close to a hit.

With more than 10,000 fans roaring on every pitch, Ryan hurled the third no-hitter of his career, tying Bob Feller's American League mark and matching Jim Maloney's National League accomplishment. Only Sandy Kofax with four ever threw more, and now Nolan was within reach of that remarkable record.

He struck out the side in the first two innings. He struck out Eric Soderholm for the last out of the last inning, and it was his 15th strikeout of the game and

367th of the season, only 16 shy of his own major-league mark. But as the press poured over him in the dressing room afterward, he sighed wearily and said, "I'll settle for this. I'm worn out."

He passed up his last start of the season, then, thus passing up a long shot at surpassing his single-season strikeout record. Perhaps significantly, he already had become the first pitcher since Bob Feller to walk more than 200 batters in a season and was passing up a chance to walk seven more and surpass Feller's single-season standard of 208.

So Nolan Ryan concluded his campaign in a blaze of glory at 22–16 with a 2.89 earned run average. He had started a personal record 41 times and completed 26 games. He had pitched a personal record 332 innings, leading the majors in both innings and strikeouts. His 367 strikeouts were the third highest single-season total ever, and he was the first ever to fan 300 or more in three seasons.

Among many new marks he put into the books were his 750 strikeouts in two successive seasons, 47 in three straight games, and 32 in two.

After a slow start the speedster had come on to capture five of his last six decisions, completing all six. After seven seasons in the majors, he finally had pushed past the .500 mark with 91 victories and 86 defeats, and 52 of those wins had come in the last three seasons. He was just approaching his peak.

Again he was passed over in the Cy Young balloting. Catfish Hunter beat out Fergie Jenkins of the Texas Rangers. Both won 25 games. But both were with winners, while Nolan was with a loser. Dick Williams said, "Nolan's twenty-two victories without much offense or defense behind him were a greater achievement than the twenty-five wins of the other two." After Catfish's contract was canceled, and he signed with the Yankees for $3,700,000 over five seasons, Williams observed, "That's nothing compared to what Ryan would be worth in the open market. He is the most precious property in sports today." Ryan signed a two-season contract for $300,000.

Ryan himself helped start rumors he would be traded. The Angels had finished last in the league in runs scored, last in double plays, and close to last in fielding. Even though they came on under Williams a little in the late stages, they still finished with the second worst record in their fourteen-year-history, 68 wins and 94 defeats, last in their division and with less than 1,000,000 in attendance.

"They have to put a team together, and the only way to do it will be to trade one of their pitchers, probably a veteran such as myself or Bill Singer. With kids coming on like Frank Tanana and Andy Hassler they may be able to sacrifice pitching for power," Nolan observed. Other teams, including the Dodgers, immediately began to pitch package offers at the Angels. But the Angels went into spring training for the 1975 season without making a move.

Owner Gene Autry said, "Nolan Ryan is becoming the greatest gate attraction in the game, and it would be unreasonable for us to let him go." General manager Harry Dalton said, "When you are losing, you have to consider anything which may make you a winner, but trading Ryan might be the worst mistake we could make." Manager Williams said, "We'll consider all offers, but I can't conceive anyone willing to give us what Ryan is worth."

Frank Robinson had been sold to Cleveland, where he would become the first black manager in the majors. Bob Oliver had been sold to Baltimore. A trade brought swift Tommy Harper from Boston to team with speedy Mickey Rivers and Morrie Nettles in what Williams hoped would become a base-stealing orgy. Moves were made to tighten the defense. "We hope to improve with our legs and gloves and what may be the best pitching staff in baseball," Williams said.

The backbone of the ball club had become Nolan Ryan, who with three no-hitters in two seasons and three 19-strikeout games in one season, had shown how suddenly his sort of lightning could illuminate the major leagues.

12 Like Lightning

Nolan Ryan, baseball's strikeout king, can strike like lightning with his fast ball at any time.

He does not do things like many pitchers. Tom Morgan, the Angel pitching coach, called Nolan his "hardest-working pitcher." He pointed out, "He is more careful about his conditioning and he throws more between starts than most pitchers." Ryan noted, "I don't dissipate much. I like to get a lot of rest, a lot of sleep. But I do work hard on the field. I'm a power pitcher, and a lot of my power comes from my legs. I run two to eight laps in the outfield before games between starts. I do stretching exercises and throw a lot to keep loose. I stand on my hands to strengthen my shoulders."

Lifting weights is not recommended for pitchers for fear they will strain muscles, tire their arms, or become muscle-bound, but he does a lot of it, even in season. He says, "It keeps me fit and strong." Also, swimming is not recommended for athletes because it is tiring and supposedly softens the skin, but Nolan swims in his pool at home, especially after games. "It keeps me from getting stiff and relaxes me," he says. Most pitchers soak their arm in ice after games. Nolan does not, asking trainer Freddy Frederico only for light rubdowns.

Ryan practices some yoga as part of his handstands and stretching exercises. While standing on his head, with his feet braced against an outfield wall, he once explained that he practiced it physically because it relaxed him but did not practice it mentally. "I'm not fully into it," he commented. "But I do some of it. If people want to laugh, let 'em. You do what helps you."

Usually fastball pitchers have been taller or heavier or had longer arms than Ryan. But the powerful push he gets from his strong legs, his unusual arm speed, and loose, snapping wrist propel the ball with tremendous velocity. He says he used to take his speed for granted, but has spent a lot of time lately trying to figure out where it comes from in order to protect it. He does not believe he has unusual arm strength, yet admits he seldom loses in arm wrestling or wrist wrestling, no more than he does in leg wrestling. Elastic muscle and natural coordination contribute to his power.

In boxing some muscular men have been light hitters, some skinny guys knockout artists. It is the same in pitching. The ones who can throw the ball the fastest do not always look the part.

Ryan is a knockout pitcher. He has suffered from those blisters on the fingers of his pitching hand, from sore elbows, from sore leg muscles, and from an aching back, but he has not suffered from a sore arm as such.

Former Red Sox manager Eddie Kasko says, "Sometimes Ryan beats himself. With walks and wild pitches. By not fielding his position well. By letting men get on base and then throwing too hard. By not holding the runners on base and permitting steals and then coming in with the ball and giving up a hit when it hurts the most."

Former Angel manager Del Rice says, "He has a fluid delivery, but his motion was awkward when he arrived with the Angels. The first time I saw him he almost fell off the mound delivering pitches he was throwing so hard. It was impossible for him to have control or to field his position properly. He is improving in that he's grooved in a reasonable rhythm and motion more now."

Ryan says, "I am maturing. I'm learning to play my position. I used to think with my fastball I had to put on a show for the fans. I was conscious of being compared to Koufax. I threw every ball as hard as I could. When I needed to make an impression or got in trouble, I tried to throw even harder. I got all out of kilter. I don't think about Koufax now. I try to be me. I have learned that I don't have to throw as hard as I can to still throw faster balls than the next guy. I can relax and throw in rhythm and throw fast but with improved accuracy. If I get into a wild streak, I try to relax even more. But I still suffer wild spells that make me tense.

"I throw my fastball about eighty percent of the time and my curveball about twenty percent. My curveball is getting better, and when it's at its best and I'm getting it over, I'll throw the fastball about seventy percent and the curveball about thirty percent. I'd like to master a change-up. Ideally I'd like to throw about sixty percent fastballs, about thirty percent curveballs, and about ten percent change-ups.

"The batters always expect fastballs from me. If I'm getting my curveball over the plate for strikes, they're in trouble. I'll have the batters off-balance. My fastball will look faster late in a game and it probably will be faster. I'll be stronger late in games and probably last longer.

"The more I pitch, the more I get grooved, the more control I should have. I have to cut down on the number of pitches I throw. It'll make me stronger. And every time I walk someone on I've put myself on a spot. He's a potential run. A single doesn't hurt you by itself unless you've put men in scoring position in front of it.

"I'd like to fire my fastball by all of 'em, but some guys hit my fastballs better than curveballs. You have to pitch smart. The smart hitters trouble me the most. With my speed, the free-swinging sluggers don't usually hurt me. It's the singles hitters, the guys who choke up on the bat and just try to get a piece of the ball and hit it anywhere who come up with the hits that hurt me.

"I don't deliberately try for strikeouts. To strike out a man, you have to throw at least three pitches. You may throw many more. To get an out, you sometimes have to throw only one. It takes too much out of your arm to throw around two hundred pitches a game. And while the records are nice, it's the victories that matter. Throwing smarter instead of trying to overpower hitters, I have a better chance for victories. So I'm not looking to surpass my records or anyone else's. But if

149

I get close to a big one, I'll probably go for it. It's in my nature, I guess. I hope to do a lot in baseball before I'm through."

Success has spoiled many athletes. It appears Ryan is a stable young man with good sense, who is not going to get carried away by his fame. He has had hard times establishing himself, his desire is still high, and he is well aware he has not yet done as well as he can do. Young yet, he remains erratic and subject to spells of wildness. But he is working hard to achieve consistency. And his many admirers are convinced he will.

At his best, he is the best. His no-hitters dramatically illustrate this and demonstrate the excitement he can produce.

The first came in Kansas City's modernistic outdoor arena under the floodlights before more than 12,000 fans on the night of May 15, 1973. Ryan hadn't won a game in two weeks and had been shelled in his last start, but just when you give up on him, he gives you a gem.

A single by Vada Pinson, a sacrifice, a fly ball, and a walk were followed by singles by Bob Oliver and Al Gallagher to give Ryan a 2–0 cushion before he faced the Royals for the first time in the last half of the first inning.

Little leadoff batter Freddie Patek struck out swinging. Steve Hovley walked and stole second. He would be the only Royal runner to reach second base all night. He was stranded there. Amos Otis struck out swinging. And Big John Mayberry took a called third strike.

In the second Cookie Rojas lined to second baseman Sandy Alomar, Ed Kirkpatrick bounced out to the pitcher, and Lou Piniella took a "K," called. In the third, Paul Schaal took a called third strike, Carl Taylor drew a walk, but Patek struck out swinging, and Hovley tapped back to the pitcher.

In the fourth Otis and Rojas flied out to right around a swinging strikeout of Mayberry. The following frame Kirkpatrick flied to center, Piniella flied to right, and Schaal fanned, swinging. In the sixth Oliver's homer made it 3–0. In the home half, Taylor struck out swinging, Patek flied to center, and Hovley bounced to short.

The fans in the stands started to stir. Under "Hits" on the home side of the scoreboard, a big "0" was starting to loom large. In the seventh Otis grounded out to short, Mayberry missed a swing at a third strike, and Rojas flied out to right, the crowd roaring with every out now.

In the broadcasters' booth, Dick Enberg and the other Angel announcers, sending the game back home on radio and television, were starting to speak with excitement. The tension was increasing. The excitement was enormous entering the eighth.

Kirkpatrick struck out swinging. Ryan had struck out at least one man each inning. Piniella flied to right. There hadn't been a ball grounded or flied to left the entire game. Working hard on Schaal, Ryan gave up his third walk. Gail Hopkins pinch-hit for Taylor. In the infield Rudy Meoli moved up on him. Second baseman Sandy Alomar motioned him back.

Hopkins got a small piece of a curveball and looped it to left-center. As Meoli raced back for it and Valentine raced in for it, it looked for a split second as if it would fall in. Almost everyone stopped breathing briefly. Valentine couldn't get to it. But with his back to the infield, Meoli stuck his glove out as far as he could, and the ball landed in the webbing of his glove.

An enormous roar went up from the crowd, and Ryan sighed with relief and strode off. "If I hadn't been moved back, I'd never have made it," Meoli said later. Ryan said, "You need help from your fielders to pitch a no-hitter. It wouldn't have been much of a hit, but it doesn't take much to spoil a no-hitter. I was thinking about it then. I wanted it. I made up my mind to throw almost all fastballs the final inning. If they hit me, they were going to hit my best."

The last of the ninth unfurled. Patek popped a pitch foul to the right of the Royal dugout, and first baseman Jim Spencer moved under it and caught it to cheers. Ryan went to two balls and two strikes on Hovley before he blazed one to him, which the batter missed with a desperate swing. The fans hollered. Even the enemy fans were for him now.

Two out. A dangerous hitter, Amos Otis, up. The excitement was electric. Ryan reared back and blazed a fast one past him. He took it for strike one to the cheers of the crowd. Ryan reared back and blazed another fast one at him. Otis swung at this one and drove it deep to right. The crowd was standing, screaming, as Ken Berry, who had entered the game for defensive purposes, went back, back, back . . . and caught the ball a few feet from the wall.

Bedlam broke out in the arena as Ryan's teammates swept over him with smiles and congratulations and the Royals limped off a beaten bunch.

Two months later, July 15, a Sunday afternoon in Detroit's ancient Tiger Stadium and a telecast back to Southern California: There were more than 44,000 fans on hand, lured by Cap Day, including many kids, and they made a tremendous racket, which grew in intensity as the dazzling day wore on.

In the opening inning Jim Northrup flied out to left, Mickey Stanley watched the blur of a called third strike whiz past him, Gates Brown walked, but Norm Cash fanned, swinging. In the second Duke Sims, Dick Mc-Auliffe, and Dick Sharon all went down swinging at ferocious rising fastballs.

In the Angel third, singles by Art Kusnyer and Sandy Alomar and a fly ball by Vada Pinson produced a run for Ryan off Jim Perry. In the home half Ellie Rodriguez and Northrup took called third strikes around a fly ball to center by Brinkman. In the fourth Stanley walked, but Brown, Cash, and Sims all struck out swinging.

Interest was rising early, not only in the no-hitter, which was young yet, but in the strikeout pace, which was near record proportions. When McAuliffe fanned, swinging, in the fifth, the fans started to holler. Sharon walked, but Rodriguez struck out, swinging. Brinkman bounced to short.

The sixth now. Northrup hit the ball sharply, but to Berry in center. Stanley whiffed with a big swing. Brown walked. But Cash grounded out to second. The seventh: Sims, McAuliffe, and Sharon struck out swinging, and the fans and the announcers were starting to scream.

Ryan had not only a no-hitter going, but 16 strikeouts through seven innings, with the record of 19 well within reach.

However, in the eighth, the Angels batted for a half hour, scoring five times. This built Ryan a 6–0 lead but left his arm cold and stiff. He admits, "I was worried going out to pitch the last two innings."

Rodriguez grounded to third to open the home half. Brinkman watched a called third strike go past. Northrup hit the ball into the air in center, and as Berry bagged it, the arena resounded with the cheers of the fans who wanted to see the young speedballer make history for them.

The teams went to the last of the ninth, Nolan tiring. The strikeout record was out of reach of his weary arm. Stanley bounced the ball to Meoli at short, and he threw the runner out to tremendous cheering. Big Gates Brown moved in. He smashed a pitch on a line to left. "My heart sank. I thought it would go through, a hit," Ryan admitted later. But the rising shot was right at Meoli, who leaped and caught it in his glove. "I thought it might be above me, but I was happy to have it," he said later. Ryan sighed as the fans yelled.

Veteran Norm Cash came up carrying a piano leg. It was for laughs. "Aren't you going to examine my bat?" he asked the home plate umpire. Ron Luciano did and advised him to substitute a better bat. Cash did, but with one ball and two strikes, all he could do with it was pop it to short left. Meoli moved back and squeezed it. Bedlam!

"Greatness," Rudy May said later, admiring Ryan. "Just greatness."

Nolan Ryan's third no-hitter came with stunning suddenness in his last start of the 1974 season. He had started the season slowly. At midseason he was struggling. By season's end he was surging. He already had struck out 19 batters in three different games during

154

the season. He already had pitched his fifth nine-inning one-hitter and fifth two-hitter, but another no-hitter had eluded him.

Minnesota was in town in a situation similar to the previous season when they came in to climax Nolan's bid for a single-season strikeout record. Now the strikeout record was just out of his reach for this season, but another no-hitter is always within the reach of this remarkable pitcher any time he takes the mound. The writers and fans are always thinking of the possibility when he pitches.

There were fewer than 11,000 fans in sprawling Anaheim Stadium for this otherwise-meaningless late-season game. Ryan started swiftly, striking out Steve Brye swinging and Rod Carew on a called third strike. He walked Steve Braun, but Bobby Darwin struck out swinging. In the second inning Ryan walked Tony Oliva but struck out Larry Hisle, Pat Bourque, and Luis Gomez in succession, the first two swinging, the third called.

In the third Glenn Borgmann flied out. Brye and Carew walked, but Braun flied out, and Darwin took a called third strike. In the fourth Oliva grounded out. Hisle walked. Bourque fanned with a big final cut. Gomez bounced out. In the Angel halves of the third and fourth the home side scored twice each time, and Ryan now had a 4–0 lead to work on.

In the fifth Borgmann bounced out. Brye and Carew walked, but Braun grounded out, and Darwin took a called third strike. Interest was stirring in the stadium. In the sixth Oliva grounded out, Hisle fanned swinging, and Bourque took a called third one. In the seventh pinch hitter Eric Soderholm, Borgmann, and Brye all flied out. Now the fans were hollering on every out, and the pressure was pounding at the pitcher.

Now the eighth inning. Carew came up, on his way to his third straight league batting championship. Carew struck out swinging. Braun struck out swinging. Big Bob Darwin moved in, hit the ball, but in the air to center. The noise seemed to swallow up Ryan as he ran into the dugout. The Angels went down in their half.

Now the ninth. Dangerous Oliva moved in. He hit the ball to center, caught, for the first out. Now Hisle. Taking desperate cuts, he struck out swinging for the third time in the game. Old Harmon Killebrew, the home-run hitter, pinch-hit. Working carefully, Ryan walked him. Then Soderholm. He took his swings. When he missed for the third strike, the arena erupted in noise, and Ryan's teammates swarmed all over him to congratulate him.

Later he sat in the dressing room, surrounded by the writers with their pads and pens, the broadcasters with their microphones and tape recorders, the photographers with their cameras popping flashbulbs in his smiling, sweating face, and he said, as unemotionally as ever, "Well, you know, it's really a nice way to wind up a long season."

As time went on, however, the seasons did not seem to grow longer to Nolan Ryan.

It was June 1, 1975, and the season scarcely seemed to have started to Ryan. That Sunday afternoon the opponents were the tough Baltimore Orioles. The Angels had been hitting weakly most of the season, but it was a day when Ryan was putting it all together. When

156

he missed with his fastball, his curve was perfect. And with those he mixed a changeup that had the Orioles gnawing their bats. The Angels scored only one run, but that was enough.

Ryan survived a seventh inning when he walked one, and another reached first on an error. When he went to the mound in the ninth, the crowd was on its feet— and stayed there, cheering every pitch. A fly out to left field, a bounce out to second. And then, facing Bobby Grich, Ryan struck him out.

Nolan Ryan had pitched his fourth no-hitter, tying Sandy Koufax's record. Where would it end?

Index

158

159

160